Epigr

"The quest for upgrading humans, creating superintelligence and godhood, is very ancient, and, in its contemporary form—dressed up in the language of advanced computer technology—very alluring."[1]

—John Lennox, Ph.D.

---

[1] John Lennox, Ph.D., *2084: Artificial Intelligence and the Future of Humanity* (Grand Rapids: Zondervan Reflective, 2020), p. 157.

Endorsement

"This book is fantastic and extremely important. This book covers lots of ground, shedding light on important topics that desperately need clear-eyed examination, individually and as a whole. In these pages, you will find biblical inspection and analysis of Darwinian evolution, transhumanism, materialism, scientism, post-humanity, and, of course, the rejection of the God of the Bible and in His replacement with fabricated man-made gods.

—Otis Graf, Ph.D.

WHO WILL RULE THE COMING 'GODS'?

THE LOOMING SPIRITUAL CRISIS OF ARTIFICIAL INTELLIGENCE

WALLACE B. HENLEY

FOREWORD AND ADDITIONAL TEXT BY
OTIS GRAF, PH.D., AEROSPACE ENGINEERING
IBM, NASA APOLLO 8 MOON PROJECT,
AND THE SPACE SHUTTLE

VIDE

Unless otherwise notated, Scriptures are taken from the New American Standard Bible® NASB. Copyright © 1960, 1971, 1977, 1995, 2020 by The Lockman Foundation. All rights reserved.

Scriptures marked NLT are taken from the Holy Bible, New Living Translation. Copyright © 1996, 2004, 2015 by Tyndale House Foundation. Used by permission of Tyndale House Publishers, Inc., Carol Stream, Illinois 60188. All rights reserved.

Scriptures marked NIV are taken from the Holy Bible, New International Version®, NIV®. Copyright © 1973, 1978, 1984, 2011 by Biblica, Inc.® Used by permission. All rights reserved worldwide.

Scriptures marked ESV are taken from the Holy Bible, English Standard Version. ESV®. Text Edition: 2016. Copyright © 2001 by Crossway Bibles, a publishing ministry of Good News Publishers.

Scriptures marked KJV are taken from the King James Version of the Bible. Public domain.

Vide Press
6200 Second Street
Washington D.C. 20011
www.VidePress.com

ISBN: 978-1-954618-37-4

Printed in the United States of America

Dedicated to Dr. Ernest Liang, Ph.D.,
University of Chicago
Founder and Director,
Center for Christianity in Business,
Houston Baptist University

Contents

Foreword

By Otis Graf, Ph.D.
Aerospace Engineering

Almost every time we press a key on a computer keyboard, touch the screen of a "smart" device, or make an audible request of Google or Alexa, we are interacting with what is called "artificial intelligence."

The use of the acronym "AI" is ubiquitous and so is AI's impact on our everyday lives. It's like home electricity. We unconsciously depend on it always being there while not realizing it is contingent on a huge non-visible infrastructure.

In the case of Alexa deciphering and acting on our request, there are data centers scattered all across the globe and high-speed interconnected data networks with trillions and trillions of bytes of data, all of which are replicated at distributed locations for backup, and hundreds of thousands of people working in a handful of huge corporations that are out of the control of any single national government.

In 2019, the *New York Times* reported that the four big tech companies–Apple, Amazon, Facebook, and Alphabet (Google's parent company)–would together generate almost a trillion dollars in revenue—an amount that rivals the GDP of countries like Saudi Arabia and the Netherlands. The total U.S. federal tax revenue will be about three trillion dollars.

The revenue of the four tech companies is increasing about 25 percent per year. Because of issues concerning how those companies secure user data and filter user speech, there has been much political clamor for increased government regulation of the "tech companies." But in the coming decade as their combined revenue surpasses that of any nation on Earth, who will regulate who? Will we have a new Caesar—a global Caesar? That seems almost inevitable.

This new age began to emerge in the late 1980s and early 1990s with the arrival of several key technologies:

- **Distributed Computing** – Information-processing jobs could be spread among a few or many networked computers.
- **The Internet** – The network was extended across the entire United States and the world.
- **Massive Data-Storage Capabilities** – "Disk Farms" were built that could store trillions and trillions of bytes of data. Data densities on storage devices increased exponentially.
- **Universal Data-Exchange Protocols** – These protocols were hammered out in international consortiums (generally dominated by U.S. organizations) and allowed anybody to exchange information with anyone else who was attached to the internet.

Research and development of artificial intelligence, including theory, software, and hardware, has been in progress for decades. But it was the arrival of the key technologies that allowed AI to be embedded in ubiquitous computer applications and small devices, such as smartphones, walking robots, and aerial drones, that has brought us to this new age.

The original internet protocols were developed by research agencies of the U.S. Department of Defense. The DoD's objective was a robust worldwide networking and computing capability that could withstand a nuclear attack that took out segments of the system. If such an event happened, the networked and distributed design would simply and imperceptibly shift information processing to the remaining operational components. It was quickly realized that all of the research labs of the U.S. government could benefit from sharing information and computing resources. Major research universities joined the internet, many of them having government research contracts. In the early days, it was just government labs and universities that participated. Commercialization was not even on the horizon.

In the late 1980s, I was the technical lead on several research projects in IBM's research lab in Houston. Our customers were mostly government research labs. It was apparent that our lab in Houston needed to have access to those labs via the internet. At the time, very few commercial organizations had internet access. We worked out a deal with Rice University enabling the telephone company to connect us to their "Sesquinet," thereby giving us an access point to the internet.

In those days, the internet and the data on its many attached computers was unregulated and available to all to a large extent. Federal and state governments paid for the software and data, so it was natural that it be a national resource. The sharing of code and programs resulted in an enormous increase in productivity. For example, if our group needed a program to do image processing or data reduction, I could download just what we needed from an organization that had a similar need and had already created the solution.

Those were remarkable days of sharing among all kinds of organizations, but then something sinister changed it all. Malicious people "shared" programs that instead of performing the advertised function would wipe out the data of the unsuspecting persons who downloaded them. The "computer virus" had arrived on the scene. The intent of the people who distributed the viruses was simply to destroy data and disable computers. There was no way to coerce compensation, as there is today. The perpetrators were attempting to sow damage and chaos for no apparent reason.

I remember the pastor of the church I attended at the time remarked that one of the best evidences of the truth and authority of the Bible is its accurate depiction of the "human condition." The arrival of computer viruses was a perfect example of that condition. They corrupted a good thing. The Bible tells us that humans are fundamentally depraved, meaning that because of our sinful nature, we have the potential to corrupt anything and everything that we influence. That situation goes all the way back to Adam and Eve in the Garden of Eden. Why should we expect a different outcome as people create AI and massive new technological capabilities?

In the early 90s, the enormous potential of the internet and its allied technologies became apparent to many in the computer industry. Online banking, distribution of all kinds of data and information, electronic newspapers, people working together regardless of time and locations across the world, the list went on and on. There were wonderful new possibilities, and corporations jumped into the action, leading to the "dot com" boom that almost immediately collapsed in the year 2000. The depravations of humanity also arrived full force in the form of malware, ransomware, hacking, thefts of data and software, more viruses, and on and on.

This book dares to delve into these and other concerns that might be labeled "spiritual." It covers a lot of ground, shedding light on important topics that desperately need clear-eyed examination, individually and corporately. In these pages, you will find biblical inspection and analysis of Darwinian evolution, transhumanism, materialism, scientism, post-humanity, and, of course, the rejection of the God of the Bible and His replacement with fabricated man-made gods.

You may be surprised to learn that in past decades, prescient Christian writers and observers, such as C.S. Lewis, anticipated the warnings Wallace B. Henley writes about here. In some ways, this book is an updated version of Lewis' book *Abolition of Man*. Lewis wrote of a group of elites who think of themselves as "progressives" and (somehow) know what the future of humanity should be and are determined to make everyone fall into line by following a direction that they dictate. "For the power of Man to make himself what he pleases will be the power of some men to make other men what *they* please. [...] These 'man-moulders' (*sic.*) of the new age will be armed with the powers of an omnicompetent state and an irrepressible scientific technique: we shall get a race of conditioners who really can cut out all posterity in any shape they please."[2]

Lewis called it "the power of some men over other men."

From this book, you will learn much about "worldview". Wallace says, "Worldviews spring from and produce more doctrinal systems, whether theistic or not." Indeed, they do and necessarily explicit doctrines that must be wholly

---

[2] C.S. Lewis, *The Abolition of Man* (New York: Macmillan, 1947), 36-39.

believed. C.S. Lewis observed, "Real Christianity and consistent Atheism both make demands on a man." What are the worldviews of the "Conditioners," as Lewis called them, who intend to bring about the progressive reformulation of humanity, pushing ever closer to gods made in their own image? It is true that the worldviews of the Conditioners are incoherent, a fact that has been demonstrated by many Christian thinkers.

More importantly, their worldviews express an ontology that is incomplete—that is, it does not incorporate all of reality. They are playing with "half a deck", or, as Wallace says, they have "a big hole in their thinking." Building super-smart machines with which to restructure humans and their society in a partial intellectual vacuum will lead to uncertain and perhaps unwanted outcomes, both good and bad.

From Wallace, you will also learn about "information" and "creation." There has been a revolution in how scientists understand the role that information plays in ordering the physical world we observe. Physicists and cosmologists have come to realize that information *was in existence prior to the creation of the universe*. But information needs a substrate to instantiate it.

Examples of information substrates are the DNA molecule that holds the genome and the memory chip in a USB drive that holds your photos and documents. What was the substrate for the information from which the universe was derived? First, we must note that the information content of "origins" explicitly allowed for the emergence of a physical world that produced a home for humanity—the Sun, Moon, and Earth. That demonstrates intentionality which is a property of mind. Therefore, information and its substrate were not all there was; there had to be an intentional mind.

Additionally, it all had to start somewhere, a starting point for the sequence of events that brought us about. To argue otherwise would be an attempt to invoke an infinite regress, something that cannot be rationally believed. Therefore, that intentional mind had the property of "self-existence." It was not created.

In 2006, a conference was held at Copenhagen University to explore fundamental concepts of matter and information in several scientific disciplines plus philosophy and theology. Physicist Paul Davies, one of its organizers, noted, "An alternative view is gaining in popularity: a view in which *information* is regarded as the primary entity from which physical reality is built [emphasis in original]."[3] John Wheeler, one of the 20th century's preeminent physicists, was among the originators of this idea and compressed it into the slogan, "It from Bit."[4]

Also, at the Copenhagen conference, Keith Ward, an Oxford University theologian and Fellow of the British Academy, explained the theological implications of this revolutionary new approach to reality:

> Taken together, these considerations suggest the idea of a primordial consciousness *that is ontologically prior to all physical realities*, that contains the "coded" information for constructing any possible universe, and that can apprehend and appreciate any physical universe that exists. It would certainly be a strong reason for creating a universe that might contain finite consciousnesses that could share in appreciating, and even in creating, some of the distinctive values potential in the

---

[3] Paul Davies, *Information and the Nature of Reality* (Cambridge: Cambridge University Press, 2010), 67.

[4] John Archibald Wheeler Postulates "It from Bit": History of Information

basic structure of the universe. [...] But if some notion of value is introduced, as a reason for actualizing some rather than other logically possible states, the notion of consciousness seems to be entailed. For it is consciousness that apprehends and appreciates value. *Only intelligent consciousness can have a reason for bringing about some state* [emphasis added].[5]

In Chapter 5, Wallace B. Henley convincingly shows how the concept of primordial information, described above, aligns perfectly with the mind of God as it is described in the Bible. God alone is self-existent. He alone has the property of aseity (a word you will encounter multiple times in this book). Philosopher William Lane Craig explains the importance of God's aseity and how it is linked to creation:

Even God could not create a self-existent being, for a created, self-existent being is as logically incoherent as a round triangle or a married bachelor. To be self-existent is to be uncreated. So, anything apart from God is a created being and therefore not self-existent. Aseity is thus an incommunicable attribute of God. God alone is self-existent; everything else is dependent for its existence upon something else. Thus, *the doctrine of divine aseity is closely related to the doctrine of creation*. According to that doctrine, everything that exists (other than God) has been created by God. So, everything that exists other than God is a created thing [emphasis added].[6]

The Bible explicitly declares God's self-existence. When Moses encountered God in the burning bush, he asked God,

---

[5] Davies, 289.

[6] How Free is God? - R. L. Kuhn | Interview | Reasonable Faith.org.

"Suppose I go to the Israelites and say to them, 'The God of your fathers has sent me to you,' and they ask me, 'What is his name?' Then what shall I tell them?" God replied to Moses with a profound assertion, "*I am who I am*. This is what you are to say to the Israelites: '*I am* has sent me to you.'" With that assertion, God declares His self-existence, and as William Lane Craig has demonstrated, every other entity is necessarily dependent on God for its existence.

And that brings us to transcendence. Self-existence and aseity result in transcendent Being. Wallace notes, "Transcendence means that which is 'above' people and the material world ... True transcendence is not an object. It has Being beyond all that exists and does not exist as one among many or several."

Transcendence, self-existence, and aseity are tightly associated non-physical attributes. Those three essences, when put up against the AI machines and the people who make them, reveal *a true crisis of our age*. That is what this book is about. The machines are not aware of anything beyond themselves; they are not even aware of their makers. However, their makers *can* contemplate something (that is, a transcendence) beyond themselves and their physical environment, but they have rejected it. In Romans chapter one, the Apostle Paul tells us:

> For although they knew God, they neither glorified him as God nor gave thanks to him, but their thinking became futile and their foolish hearts were darkened. Although they claimed to be wise, they became fools and exchanged the glory of the immortal God for images made to look like a mortal human being and birds and animals and reptiles. (Romans 1:21-23, NIV)

When there is a loss of a sense of transcendence, there is no inclination to ask the question, "Who decides?" People forget the importance of that question when they pretend there is no almighty God and no authority above themselves. As Wallace puts it, "What will artificial intelligence regard as having transcendent authority over it?" Without a transcendent God, it is only ourselves (or the machines) who decide. This is an old story. The Bible's book of Judges tells us, "Everyone did what was right in his own eyes" (Judges 21:25). As Wallace noted, the Bible also tells us that there are other eyes that we need to be aware of:

> The eyes of the Lord are everywhere,
> keeping watch on the wicked and the good.

That awareness of a higher, transcendent authority other than ourselves is the only brake on destructive human ambitions. All the destructive secular ideologies of the last century and the current one can be de-legitimized by asking the question, "Who decided that?" The only answer is, "Those with the most power and influence." That prompts a follow-on question, "Then why should we do as they say?" Wallace frames the issue this way, "Our contention in this book is that it is not so much the machines about which we should be concerned, but the people, their worldviews, moral and ethical values, and especially spiritual principles that they bring to their work."

And then there are the manufactured gods. Wallace discusses the "rise of the 'god factories'." Humans are an idol-making species. God's warnings against idols are pervasive in the Bible. Forward-thinking AI makers envision machines with seemingly god-like powers. Compared to the motionless stone carvings of years past, those machines will have real-world powers. They will be ever so helpful, offering enormous productivity and prosperity. But given our history of idol-making, we can expect that they may play a larger role. Wallace asks, "What is it that human creators will 'breathe' into the artificial intelligence machines they will construct? Why would we build machines that become our lords and masters and jettison the true God of transcendent love and holiness?"

This book lays out a comprehensive description of the future world that our godless technological and enormously rich elites envision. But what should be the response of God-fearing people? That is the important message of this book. Paraphrasing Chuck Colson and Francis Schaeffer, "How then shall we live?" The answer to that question requires biblical knowledge, relying on God's revealed word. We must return to the Bible. Wallace's book will be an indispensable resource to Christians as a guide to the proper use of all of the multiple interfaces in the world of AI and its pervasive technologies.

Jesus said that we are to be "in the world" and not "of the world." While it is still in the world, one of the roles of the church is to speak clearly with a prophetic voice—a voice that is emphatically directed to "the world." That is not "prophecy" as in terms of predicting future events. Instead, it is rather a "forth-telling" of the certain outcomes that follow when humanity rejects God, ignores His written word, and violates His biblical commands on how we must order our lives. In that sense, this book is prophetic.

If the Bible is true, then we should expect to witness certain outcomes in world history, and we should anticipate prophetic voices to arise in the church who will speak warnings of those outcomes. That is what is happening with Wallace B. Henley and this book. It will be valuable to Christians so they know what to expect and will have an understanding of the progression of events in the near future.

This book also has the potential to open the minds of non-Christians, even secularists and atheists, so they gain some awareness of the risks inherent in the existence of unimaginably powerful technologies in the hands of enormously rich global organizations that are populated by people who have no sense of a transcendent higher authority.

Some might not like the analyses provided in this book and may disagree with some of what Wallace has to say, but I am convinced that it is not possible to rationally demonstrate that these analyses are wrong. Anyone, regardless of their worldview, will profit from considering the arguments presented in this book.

—Otis Graf, Ph.D.
Houston, Texas

Author's Preface

The people are strong and tall—descendants of
the famous Anakite giants. You have heard the saying,
"Who can stand up to the Anakites?"
—Deuteronomy 9:2, NLT

The bolt that morning seemed to burst through the ceiling and walls of the Cracker Barrell where Dr. Ernest Liang and I were breakfasting.

It was not a literal flash of lightning, but a burst of insight as Dr. Liang talked.

Ernest is one of the world's top experts in finance, and he was talking about the rapid expansion and dangers of an increasingly wired global economy. Dr. Liang is not an extremist. His credentials include a Ph.D. from one of the premiere schools of finance in the world—the University of Chicago—and years of experience in corporate life. I pulled closer and listened carefully.

I suddenly became aware of how vulnerable humanity will be as the machines seem increasingly godlike in an age when people are rejecting beliefs in God as the Transcendent Being to Whom all are accountable and giving the contraptions of their own making an almost godlike power and position.

Who or what will control all of this? To what values and worldviews will the machines be programmed to submit? In the final analysis, will they obey their human masters, or will human beings become the *mastered*?

As I left our breakfast meeting, my mind was reeling. I thought of George Orwell and his chilling 1949 novel, *Nineteen Eighty-Four,* where he described a grimly authoritarian world controlled by a continual electronic presence called "Big Brother." Nineteen eighty-four was the year Orwell fixed for the appearance of such a society. Though this dystopian future did not arrive that year, Orwell's prediction could well become true. Futurist Ray Kurzweil, Google's director of engineering, says, "I have set the date 2045 for the 'Singularity' which is when we will multiply our effective intelligence a billion-fold by merging with the intelligence we have created."[7]

In 1993, mathematician and science fiction writer Vernon Vinge told a symposium, "Within thirty years we will have the technological means to create superhuman intelligence." Not long after that breakthrough, "the human era will be ended."[8]

This "superhuman intelligence" that will increasingly displace humanity is the "Singularity" Kurzweil predicts. It will be "a future period in which technological change will be so rapid and its impact so profound that every aspect of human life will be irreversibly transformed." Technology will give rise to the Singularity as we reach "a point in the near future when technology will be changing so rapidly that we will have to

---

[7] Kurzweil Claims That the Singularity Will Happen by 2045 (futurism.com)
[8] "The Coming Technological Singularity: How to Survive in the Post-Human era," by Vernor Vinge. © 1993 by Vernor Vinge. Retrieved from https://edoras. sdsu.edu/~vinge/misc/singularity.html, December 12, 2018.

enhance ourselves with artificial intelligence to keep up," Kurzweil believes.

In that new age, there will be "no clear distinction between humans and machines." The computers will not be merely in our pockets and purses, but "inside our bodies and brains," so that "we're going to be a hybrid of biological and non-biological intelligence."[9]

And, according to some students of AI, the machines will be "above" us as well—like a god. Kurzweil's remarks are found on a website with the address, transcendentman.com (which says it all).

But as we will argue in this book, it won't be the human that is transcendent, but the machine.

Yet some believe this breakthrough that Vinge and Kurzweil forecast will usher in a utopian world where "we will be billions of times more intelligent and there will be no clear distinction between human and machine, real reality and virtual reality. Human aging and illness will be reversed, world hunger and poverty will be solved, and we will ultimately cure death."[10]

"BRAVE NEW WORLD"

But what about people in societies not as technologically advanced as Silicon Valley? In *Brave New World,* Aldous Huxley's classic describing another form of dystopia, there is a crass, intentional effort to make sure everyone stays in their place as allotted by the "Predestinators." Humans are seeded by artificial insemination, developed in lab bottles rather than

---

[9] "What is the Singularity, and when will the Singularity occur?" Retrieved from https://transcendentman.com/when-singularity-occur, December 12, 2018.
[10] *Ibid.*

human wombs, and conditioned for the roles they are to play in society—the "Alphas" at the top, the "Epsilons" as the servant classes, and variations in between.

Will the coming of the Singularity and its "brave new world" widen the gap between the "haves" and the "have nots"? Will there be missionary movements of the transhumans trying to convert the still fully humans into the new transhumanist nature?

Will people who don't want to be converted be allowed to refuse? Or will they be regarded as deterrents to the unstoppable progression of evolution and the survival of the fittest?

THE DEPRIVED

Worse, will the deprived of the world be like those in Huxley's *Brave New World* who are bred and conditioned by the "Predestinators" to be "Epsilons", as declared by the Director of Hatcheries and Conditioning in Huxley's grim world as not needing "human conditioning"?[11]

The spoiler that will turn this utopia into dystopia is the nature of the fallen human being, which no machine can fix. The reality from the Garden of Eden to this moment and the future is that *whatever has dominion (transcendence) over the human being will determine how the human being exercises his or her God-given dominion over nature and the world.*

That means True Transcendence is the most important issue of our time, leading to some disturbing questions:

---

[11] Aldous Huxley, *Brave New World* (New York: HarperCollins Publishers, 2017), 13-15.

- Will it be the transcendence of God or the machine?
- What is transcendent for the creators of artificial intelligence, guiding their personal ethics and setting the ethical boundaries they program into the machines?
- Will the new humanity inhabit a lustrous "new Eden," or will it be a world of cold authoritarianism under the glaring mechanical eyes of an AI "god"?

These are questions we probe in this book and which humanity must face as we zoom toward 2024.

I do not come to the writing of this book as an academic or scholar, but as a reporter. My first daily newspaper job was in 1966, the evening of the golden age of journalism. I am still a reporter. I cite many references in these pages, seeking to bring into view the work and thought of people developing the AI mechanisms that may be treated like gods in a fast-approaching future. Conveying the thoughts of others into public view is the work of the reporter. This is my aim.

The greatest honor in life and vocation is to be a reporter of the Good News, the Gospel of Jesus Christ and His Kingdom. I hope that as you sort through the details presented here, you will also find many reasons for hope.

—Wallace B. Henley

The Coming "Gods"

What is going to be created will effectively be a god... (If) there is something a billion times smarter than the smartest human, what else are you going to call it?

—Anthony Levandowski[12]

I look at my grandchildren and great-grandchildren and wonder what kind of future they will inhabit. Perhaps you do the same. One thing for certain, our offspring are coming into an age of crisis regarding transcendence.

It stunned me a while back when I realized there is more technology in my home office than on Air Force One—the President's airplane—in the 1970s when I was working in the Nixon White House. Georgetown University's Dr. Joshua Mitchell notes, "(T)he computing power of a common smartphone exceeds the computing power the astronauts of Apollo 11 had at their disposal during the first manned landing on the

---

[12] "Inside the First Church of Artificial Intelligence," By Mark Harris, *Wired,* November 15, 2017. Retrieved from https://www.wired.com/story/anthony-levandowski-artificial-intelligence-religion/, July 21, 2018.

moon in 1969."[13] Professor Luigi Zingales of the University of Chicago points out:

> We have at our fingertips today more advanced hard-ware and computing power than was used to send man to the moon, more information than is contained in the best library, and more power to communicate than any propaganda machine ever dreamed of possessing.[14]

And, I would add, there is a growing number of technological geniuses like Anthony Levandowski who believe we humans now have so much power available to us that we can create "god." The Bible says that God created us in His image, but now, having lost the vision of True Transcendence, some are attempting to make "god" in the human image. We explore this in Chapter Seven.

Humanity's endless preoccupation with self, beginning in the Garden of Eden, has reached critical mass. The sense of God's transcendence has been eclipsed in the hearts of the multitudes by fascinations on the immanent scale. Humanity is so enthralled by the horizontal that it forgets to look up to the vertical, "The Lord high and lifted up," in Isaiah's words (Isaiah 6:1-6).

We examine the crisis of transcendence in Chapters Two, Three, and Four. We will discover that the dangers for us, our families, and civilization are immense. The existential crisis is that *in the very age when the recognition of and reverence for the transcendence of God is being eclipsed, technology is on the verge of dramatic breakthroughs in robotics.* In the rush to

---

[13] Joshua Mitchell, *American Awakening: Identity Politics and Other Afflictions of Our Time* (New York: Encounter Books, 2020) xii.

[14] "Should We Regulate Big Tech?" by Luigi Zingales (*Imprimis: A Publication of Hillsdale College,* November, 2018, Vol.47, No.11), 2.

make artificial intelligence machines better serve us humans, the wizards of the cyberworld are making machines that many predict will master us. As we will see, some people are already worshiping at the feet of the great god of AI, just as the ancient Philistines once bowed before statues of the idol Dagon.

We have nothing to fear if the human creators of artificial intelligence mechanisms are themselves aware of their accountability before the true God for the gifts, talents, and skills He has given them for glorifying Him and serving His creation. But if the AI designers see only on the immanent scale, if their motives, moral values, and ultimate ends are focused only on the horizontal, there is much about which to be concerned.

In the effort to give us utopia, they will bring us into dystopia. Thus, John Burger's question is again haunting, "Will Big Data and artificial intelligence usher in Orwell's Vision of 1984?"[15]

Stephen Hawking foresaw the possibility of such an Orwellian age (as well as the "Brave New World" described by Aldous Huxley). Hawking warned there could arise in the future a rich, elitist class who had the wherewithal to manipulate the DNA of their offspring. Though there might be laws passed against such genetic engineering, it would be hard for some with means to resist the temptation to modify the humans they beget.

A two-tiered society would result—the "superhuman" and the "unimproved." This would lead to "significant political

---

[15] "Will Big Data and artificial intelligence usher in Orwell's Vision of 1984? By Jon Burger, March 15, 2017. Retrieved from https://aleteia.org/2017/03/15/will-big-data-and-artificial-intelligence-usher-in-orwells-vision-of-1984/, August 3, 2018.

problems because the 'unimproved' people won't be able to compete." The lower tier would die off, leaving a race of "self-designing beings who are improving at an ever-increasing rate" and who then "spread out and colonize other planets and stars."

Artificial intelligence would facilitate this "improving" of the race. Ultimately, it could displace even the improved humanity. "AI could develop a will of its own, a will that is in conflict with ours and which could destroy us," Hawking told an audience of technologists at the Web Summit in 2017.[16] "We stand on a threshold of a brave new world," he said. That world, Hawking predicted, will need "effective management in all areas of its development."[17]

Hawking was echoing Huxley and Orwell. Others have joined in that concern, like Lionel Trilling, the twentieth-century literary critic who also saw the similarities between Orwell's fictional world and developments in the actual world. Trilling concluded that Orwell was not writing only about the Russian police state that had developed in that era under the communists but was actually giving "the image of the impending future" and showing that "the ultimate threat to human freedom may well come from a similar and even more massive development of the social idealism of our democratic culture."[18]

---

[16] This was billed as "the largest tech conference in the world," bringing together 60,000 tech specialists to listen to 1,200 speakers. The meeting was in Lisbon, Portugal.

[17] "Stephen Hawking predicted a race of superhumans will take over the world," by Nick Whigham, *news.com.au*, October 15, 2018. Retrieved from https://www.news.com.au/technology/science/human-body/stephen-hawking-predicted-a-race-of-superhumans-will-take-over-the-world/news-story/b7c3e16159aab6fae53abaaa326e61c2, December 5, 2018.

[18] Cited in Gertrude Himmelfarb, *The Moral Imagination* (Chicago: Ivan R. Dee, 2006) 227.

Trilling thought the "essential point" of Orwell's book was "the danger of the ultimate and absolute power which mind can develop when it frees itself from conditions, from the bondage of things and history."[19] *The greatest danger, as we will argue in this book, comes when the human mind is untethered from True Transcendence.*

We don't call here for the minds of AI developers to be placed in bondage, but we warn of the lure into the danger of ultimate and absolute power for the human mind that does not recognize and respect the boundaries of transcendent values.

In *The Abolition of Man,* CS Lewis wrote, "Man's conquest of nature, if the dreams of some scientific planners are realized, means the rule of a few hundreds of men (and women) over billions and billions of men (and women)."[20]

Satya Nadella, Microsoft CEO, told the 2017 conference of computer builders, "What Orwell prophesied in *Nineteen Eighty-Four,* where technology was being used to monitor, control, dictate, or what (Aldous) Huxley imagined (in *Brave New World*) we may do just by distracting ourselves without any meaning or purpose—neither of these futures is something that we want."

But that future, Nadella suggested to the engineers in his audience, "is going to be defined *by the choices that you as developers make and the impact of those choices on the world.*"[21] Nadella may have been tardy with his exhortation to computer devel-

---

[19] Himmelfarb, 227.

[20] C.S. Lewis, *The Abolition of Man,* 1974, 58.

[21] "Microsoft CEO: tech sector needs to prevent '1984 future,' May 11, 2017. Retrieved from: https://www.news.com.au/technology/home-entertainment/computers/microsoft-ceo-tech-sector-needs-to-prevent-1984-future/news-story/eb533f55d35a8bf6d0ea4243f96b05e3, August 3, 2018. (Italics added)

opers. "The 'machine learning' algorithms that fuel so much of modern life already are inscrutable; even their designers don't really know how they form decisions."[22]

Aldous Huxley's *Brave New World* was ruled over by the "Alphas." This elite group saw to it that the people they dominated were distracted by technology and sedated by "bread and circuses." Huxley wrote of a technical aggregate that was "an assault against silence." Reflective thinking that might have led deluded people to see they were the subjects of a grand ruse would be impossible in the world of constant noise. The din, wrote Huxley, "penetrates the mind, filling it with a babel of distractions."[23]

Huxley's *Brave New World* is a book about transcendence— the absence from the experience of it from the human spirit and thus from the existential world. But it cannot be otherwise because the humans in that world imagined by Huxley are bred to have no spirits, just bodies wafting along in periodic hazes through the drug "soma" and punctuated with sexual coupling that is encouraged from toddlerhood.[24] The minds of the citizens of the "World State" are programmed, the emotions conditioned, and the wills pre-set.

The "planetary motto" of the World State is "Community, Identity, Stability," achieved through the rigidity of law and custom set by the planners who constitute the only transcendence the people of the Brave New World know.

Yet the hunger for True Transcendence is there, expressed in the plaintive cry of a newcomer to the World State. The

---

[22] "AI: The ultimate guide," by Richard Fisher, July 14, 2015. Retrieved from http://www.bbc.com/future/story/the-ultimate-guide-to-ai, August 3, 2018.
[23] Citations to come in completed manuscript.
[24] *Brave New World*, 147.

man, considered a "Savage" because, among other things, he was conceived by a father and mother in the mother's womb rather than in a bottle, is told by the World State's Controller that the compulsory style is because "we prefer to do things comfortably."

"I don't want comfort. I want God. I want poetry. I want real danger. I want goodness. I want sin," the visitor says.[25]

Rather than "Community, Identity, and Stability" as a motto for our culture, it seems our present "secular deities" are "national interest," "social justice," and "scientific progress," and their "softer variants" of "nationalism," "Marxism," and "scientism." These, writes Jakub Bozydar Wisniewski, "plague Western culture." [26]

Will the deepening of the Age of Artificial Intelligence at the very moment when the sense of True Transcendence is fading from our culture someday elicit such a cry from weary transhumans and others suffocating under avalanches of data?

Orwell's fictional world had a god-figure in Big Brother, the mouthpiece of the Party, staring out of a screen without ceasing. But apparently, the real world in the decades ahead will have its own form of "god." Former Google and Uber engineer Anthony Levandowski predicts that at some point, an

---

[25] *Brave New World,* 240. A consequence of the absence of the experience of True Transcendence is the lack of the acknowledgement of sin and repentance. Without that, humans cannot know God's grace. Huxley's character uttering that line is expressing revolt at a culture of human-contrived moralisms, enforced by stern legalisms—a society without grace because it does not have a doctrine of sin and repentance, which brings on the floods of God's grace, its peace and joy.

[26] "The Uneasy Hiatus of the Infantile era," by Jakub Bozydar Wisniewski, *The Imaginative Conservative,* December 28, 2018. Retrieved from https://theimaginativeconservative.org/2018/12/uneasy-hiatus-infantile-era-jakub-wisniewski.html, December 29, 2018.

artificial intelligence machine will have and be able to process so much data that people will call it "god." As we have seen, Levandowski believes this so passionately he has formed his AI "church" called "The Way of the Future." Its mission "is about creating a peaceful and respectful transition of who is in charge of the planet from people to people + machines (sic.)."

The AI church's founder has no doubt about the inevitability of artificial intelligence being in charge. It's only a matter of time. Thus, humanity "should think about how 'machines will integrate into society (and even have a path to being in charge as they become smarter and smarter) so that this whole process can be amicable and not confrontational.'"

There is an ominous element in Levandowski's thought. "We believe it may be important for machines to see who is friendly to their cause and who is not," he says. This will necessitate an Orwellian monitoring system. Levandowski's plan includes "keeping track of who has done what (and for how long) to help the peaceful and respectful transition" from human dominion to AI being "in charge."[27]

There is really no way to keep this from happening, says Levandowski, so we need to give up trying. In fact, "this feeling of *we must stop this* is rooted in twenty-first century anthropomorphism."[28]

"Anthropomorphism" comes from several Greek words that together mean "in the form of a man—or human." This idea stands in contrast to the nature of God, described in the word that will have central focus in this book—*transcendence*. It means that which is above people and the material world.

---

[27] Way of the Future? Worship of Artificial Intelligence – YHWH's Janitor (yhwhjanitor.com)
[28] Church of the AI God is even creepier than I imagined - CNET

Philosophers used "especially the terms the one, the good, the true, and the beautiful to describe that which transcends human life," writes Glenn W. Olsen. Theologians see the transcendent as being "identified with God and with what eventually were called supernatural realities."[29]

We can also think of the transcendent as that which lifts us above a merely human worldview and its behaviors into a higher quality of existence that comes from something other than us and of infinitely higher being. Transcendence tugs us upward into the full dimension of love, expressed in the Bible as *agape*—love without the primacy of self-interest—as well as ethics and morality that reflect the holiness of God.

Thus, transcendence and anthropomorphism stand in direct contrast at times.

The excitement in some quarters of the cyberworld regarding the manufacture of virtual human beings signals the arrival of a new age.

A major crisis of our time is that we are increasingly beguiled by virtualism and are having a hard time distinguishing the imaginary from the actual. Many cyber-dazzled people are "Clark Kents", searching for a telephone booth from which they can emerge in a cape and blue leotards to stop rushing locomotives.

We have entered a new age in which we can go into the quietness of our rooms and slip into whatever identity we desire—virtually.

---

[29] Glenn W. Olsen, *The Turn to Transcendence,* ix.

Coming into a new age is not all that novel historically. It is the pattern of history to go from one stage to another as it is the pattern of a train passing through several stations *en route* to its ultimate destination. The Bible reveals this when it speaks of various "dispensations," "seasons," or "ages".

Thus, the Western Medieval period was shoved aside by the Renaissance and from the Renaissance came the Enlightenment which gave rise to the Age of Reason which led to the Modernist Age which faded into Postmodernism.

Now, say many cultural observers, we are in the post-Postmodern period.

But what do we call it?

I suggest *The Age of Virtualism.*

We have virtual identities in the form of avatars or even appropriated ethnicity. At the time in which I write, we have virtual church, caused by the coronavirus and quarantines. People are discovering they can attend church online, not having to bother with all the messy relationships in a gathered congregation of real humans.

On a larger social scale in the Age of Virtualism, many have virtual friends in virtual neighborhoods in virtual communities. We have virtual history by which we reform the facts of the past in light of our experience of the present, producing a new narrative more suited to our existential tastes. We have virtual politics through which we assume people beautiful, rich, and famous are automatically qualified to govern.

In fact, in the Virtual Age, fame of any sort makes one a policy-sage, able to make pronouncements on foreign affairs, economic issues, immigration, and much more.

J. Warner Wallace points out that the proliferation of media, especially among the young, is threatening the metanarrative or the encompassing worldview around which people sharing a society have found their points of unity.

Mark Sayers, author of *The Road Trip that Changed the World,* believes Christianity provides "the perfect balance between transcendence and immanence." In previous generations, there was an imbalance toward transcendence to the extreme of deism, Sayers thinks. Thus, in the 1980s and 90s, "There was a kickback, a rediscovery of God's immanence." Now, however:

> There is a whole new generation of young adults coming of age who have grown up in the immanence revolution of the eighties and nineties who see God not as distant and deistic, who see God as something akin to a permissive parent, who have grown up with "cool" Christianity, who live in a secular culture which represses any idea of transcendence. Thus, we have a generation who is hungering for the transcendent, yet we have a generation of leaders still reeling from the overly transcendent view of God (as distant and deistic) that they grew up with. Getting the balance is the key.[30]

---

[30] From an interview with J.R. Woodward. Retrieved from http://jrwoodward.net/2012/05/interview-with-mark-sayers-author-of-the-road-trip-that-changed-the-world-part-3/, December 13, 2018.

Micronarratives are displacing unifying presuppositions and encompassing stories that enable a shared understanding of the reality around us. "We still love stories, but we are less likely to share the same story," says J. Warner Wallace. The outcome is threatening to any metanarrative and the values springing from it that individuals shared as a community prior to the age of media proliferation. The phenomenon "encourages us to isolate and steep ourselves in micronarratives at the expense of shared narratives," Wallace believes.[31] Where once there was unity, now there is fragmentation.

The profusion of media-enhanced micronarratives thus means more and more people are living in their own virtual worlds.

The Virtual Age even has its version of what some Bible students call the Rapture—when the church, they say, will be "caught up" into the clouds. In the Age of Virtualism, our thoughts are already stored in "the Cloud."

The Virtual Age is sensate. For Virtualists, personal feelings are the measure of reality and the good within it. In his study of historic cultures, Harvard sociologist Pitirim Sorokin found a cycle in which the sensate follows the mystical and metaphysical, then gets swept off its feet by idealism. Thus, if Postmodernism sought the spiritual, the Age of Virtualism and the passion for progressivism was sure to follow.

The Virtualist pulpit focuses on making congregations feel good about themselves. It encourages denying the negatives in life—from bad health to financial crisis, no matter how real

---

[31] "How Media consumption threatens the future of Christianity (it's not what you think)," by J. Warner Wallace, *The Christian Post*, November 13, 2018. Retrieved from https://www.christianpost.com/voice/how-media-consumption-threatens-future-christianity.html, December 13, 2018.

they are. The hard truth of sin and judgment lies back there in the dust and ash heaps of an old age long dead.

The Bible does give us hope, but it also socks us with hard reality. In a sinless virtual world, we are all pure, but the Scripture tells us that we are all like sheep that have gone astray. We have all sinned and fallen short of God's glorious image in which we were made. This is ultimate reality that the virtual world tries to escape through delusionary thinking and imagery.

In the real world, sinners need redemption. Jesus Christ comes into that gritty, bloody dimension, and through suffering that was anything but fantasy, He wins the victory for us. Our holiness in Him is not virtual, but imperishable fact that will withstand the Judgment. That is, we go from being sinners to becoming saints through our identification with Him and the embrace by faith of His atonement and resurrection.

Meanwhile, back in the Age of Virtualism, people refuse "to receive the love of the truth so as to be saved." The Lord gave them what they wanted, "God will send upon them a deluding influence so that they will believe what is false" (2 Thessalonians 2:10-12).

This desire for delusion is a perfect set-up for the anti-christ—Paul's point in this passage. The Age of Virtualism is a dangerous time in which to live. In such an age as this, we need hefty doses of truth and reality. The Word of God supplies it.

The development of artificial intelligence promises either a brilliant future or poses a threat to the very survival of humans. Much will depend on the ethical values and moral codes programmed into the machines. The human being is

Imago Dei, made in the image of God. According to the Bible, that image has been defaced by evil. Now fallen humans will construct *imago hominis,* robotics bearing the image of sin-marred humans. The fundamental issue of power is that *whatever has dominion over the individual human determines how the individual exercises his and her God-given dominion over creation.* "If AI transcends into Big Brother in a way that *appears* to be the best thing for society, I'm worried the masses will buy it without vetting," writes Lindsay Bell, a specialist in content marketing.[32]

Considering such possibilities and portents, many questions arise, such as:

- Who will rule over the new gods? (Which is another way of asking what will artificial intelligence regard as having transcendent authority over *it?*)
- Who decides the values and ethical boundaries governing the machines that might have godlike status in the future?
- Who will be the equivalent in the future of Orwell's "Party" that controls the god-like machines?
- To borrow words from C.S. Lewis in *The Abolition of Man,* are people "without chests" building artificial intelligence robots "without chests"?
- Can we really expect such devices to honor and serve us, or is it inevitable we will awaken to the terrifying reality that we have traitors in our midst of our own making?
- If the human being is made in the image of the infinite, perfect God (though that image is marred in

---

[32] "Artificial Intelligence: The Good, the Bad, and the Orwellian," by Lindsay Bell. Retrieved from https://v3b/2016/03/artificial-intelligence-good-bad-orwellian/amp.

the human by evil), will the AI machine the human creates be made in the image of finite, fallen humanity?

- Can the human be truly transcendent to the machine if the machine can become greater than the human? If a man or woman could outclass God's omniscience, then God would no longer be the singular transcendent One. Thus, Levandowski is terribly right—the machine that can become superior to its maker is the "transcendent one."

- According to Romans 2:15, God has written His laws on the human heart. But who is constructing the algorithms of ethical and moral criteria that will determine good and bad in the operating system of an AI machine?

- And the most troubling question of all, will they be controllable?

Who will rule the coming gods?

This is a crucial concern. "A programmer—someone who creates algorithms and codes them up—is a minor god, creating universes at will," writes Pedro Domingos in *The Master Algorithm*. Algorithms, he says, "can reflect a programmer's ignorance or prejudice or explicit design." Further and more ominous, "Algorithms can also learn to rewrite themselves ... they can be self-programming, introducing a degree of uncertainty into the original parameters."

This can lead to the possibility of skewed knowledge, error that can go viral, and "delusions," Domingos warns. This is "a tree whose fruit should not be plucked and eaten."[33] In the

---

[33] "Silicon Valley's Futile Search for Utopia Via the 'Perfect Algorithm,'" by David Solway, September 13, 2018. Retrieved from https://pjmedia.com/trending/silicon-valleys-futile-search-for-utopia-via-the-perfect-algorithm/. November 21, 2018.

end, the alarming discovery is that creators who seemed to be in the god-role were actually fashioning the gods at whose altars they themselves eventually had to bow.

Thus, the urgency of the core query of this book, *Who will rule the coming gods?*

Answering that question is beyond my range of knowledge, even though I have been using computers for years. In the early 1970s, I helped transition the newsroom of a large city daily from typewriters to word processors. I will never forget the Saturday evening not long after we had gone live when someone's push of a wrong button wiped out the entire Sunday morning newspaper, due on the streets in a few hours. Frantically, we had to recover the hard copies of hundreds—maybe thousands—of reports that we had held onto for security, scan them, and rebuild the entire Sunday edition.

Despite my decades at a computer keyboard, I still need much help. Irene, my wife, is amazing in her capacity to understand programs and how to make the machines work. I call her my "in-house IT department." Both of our adult children and their spouses have worked for years in computer-related industries. Our grandchildren and even our great-grandchildren are computer-savvy. Further, in the writing of this book, I have assembled a team of experts, trained specialists operating in broad segments of the cyber world.

- John Curry

John is a communicator with much experience across a variety of electronic platforms and settings. John worked 23 years in communications and external affairs for British Petroleum, managing projects and interacting with the public and government agencies, including the development of communications and coordination of crisis response. John currently manages his own company, Curry & Co., which specializes in strategic communications, maximizing internet platforms.

- Leah Faul

Leah is a top expert in interactive content marketing. She has served as the president of the Houston Interactive Marketing Association and is founder and president of *15,000 Cubits*, a strategic SEO agency that guides companies and institutions in developing and applying interactive strategies.

- Otis Graf, Ph.D.

Otis holds a Bachelor of Science degree in physics and mathematics and a Ph.D. in aerospace engineering, both from the University of Texas. He worked for NASA at the Johnson Space Flight Center on the Apollo lunar landing program and the Space Shuttle project. Otis has also done computer systems engineering work for IBM, designing data-storage systems for government and university organizations. He is a voluntary apologist for Reasons to Believe (reasons.org), an organization devoted to biblical apologetics.

- Brad Hays

Brad is a mathematician, entrepreneurial business leader, and founder of Leaven Exchange, a coaching consultancy devoted to helping business leaders implement biblical principles in their companies. Brad led two start-up technology companies as the CEO in the Automotive Aftermarket segment. Brad's automotive experience was gained during 28 years of leading large operating divisions for Honeywell International (formerly AlliedSignal) and Pennzoil.

- Marty Levine

Marty Levine holds an engineering degree from the Georgia Institute of Technology (Georgia Tech) and has been employed more than 30 years in commercial roles in the chemistry industry. The global perspectives he has obtained and his keen interest in Christian apologetics has provided Marty with unique perspectives on Christian and other worldviews.

- Ernest Liang. Ph.D.

Ernest, to whom I dedicate this book, studied economics and finance at the University of Chicago, whose school of economics was made famous by Nobel Prize winner and Chicago faculty member economist Milton Friedman. Dr. Liang spent 25 years in executive management roles in business, from start-ups to Fortune 100 companies. Dr. Liang is an associate professor of finance at Houston Baptist University, the director of HBU's Center for Christianity in Business, and an editor of the *Christian Business Review*. A major focus for Dr. Liang is the increasing domination of high-frequency trading firms in capital markets driven by artificial intelligence.

- Ozie Owen, Ph.D.

Ozie holds a Ph.D. in chemical engineering from Northwestern University. At this writing, he is the Director of Hydrocarbon Management, Global Operations Organization for British Petroleum, based in Houston. Dr. Owen makes extensive use of computer-based technology in his demanding field. He is an avid student of the Bible and teaches at his local church.

• Larry Ruddell, Ed.D.

Larry is author of *Business Ethics—Faith That Works: Leading Your Company to Long Term Success*. He holds degrees in psychology and counseling and a doctorate from the University of Houston with an emphasis on computer systems and business ethics. He is a consultant to several corporations. A commissioned chaplain in the U.S. Navy, Dr. Ruddell has served his country overseas as well as in the U.S.A.

You will also hear important voices of the past in these pages. Aldous Huxley and George Orwell wrote with striking prescience as it relates to our era. They did so because their stories were framed by the authoritarianisms of their age—Fascism and Communism. They write with such relevance for our age because these are the same authoritarianisms we grapple with now.

You will also encounter key Christian thinkers from the past who speak with even greater impact because they are prophetic. C.S. Lewis, the famed British academic and author of *The Abolition of Man*, among many other works that speak into our times, is regarded as the greatest Christian apologist (defender) of the twentieth century. Jacques Ellul, a French philosopher and professor of law at the University of Bordeaux, saw with surprising clarity in the light of our present challenges into what he called "the technological bluff" (also the title of one of his books). Romano Guardini, a philosopher, and theologian at the University of Munich in the critical postwar era in Europe, wrote perceptively of *The End of the Modern World*.

I seek to draw these past important voices and others into a conversation with the present, represented by the contemporary specialists I have listed. I make no claims to being a scholar, but I am a reporter who wants to let the brilliant thinkers of our past mingle with those of the present to make us aware of future promising possibilities of artificial intelligence. However, these same voices will warn us of the dangers of AI development in a period when shapers of the cultural consensus and its values have buried the awareness of True Transcendence in oceans of chatter and deep pits of data.

I began my career as a reporter and editor for *The Birmingham News* when that city was atremble with the civil rights revolution led by Dr. Martin Luther King. I developed a strong interest in how worldview forms societies and their cultures. In 1970, I became assistant director of the Cabinet Committee on Education at the White House and was later appointed as a presidential aide.

My interest in ethics and worldview intensified as I watched the Nixon presidency disintegrate because of scandals and cover-ups. The most important thing that happened to me in the White House was reconnecting to the faith that had been so important in my growing-up years. This happened during my participation in a weekly staff prayer group that met in the West Wing.

Ultimately, believing the Bible and the Kingdom of God revealed in its pages and the life and ministry of Jesus Christ to be the answer to the chaos and suffering I observed and wrote about, I became a pastor. I also traveled extensively in the former Soviet Bloc after the collapse of communism, working with church leaders seeking to anchor their turbulent nations as they thrust off the bondage of Marxist dictatorships. I especially remember teaching an ethics workshop in a major Soviet city and how ethics was a new topic for those who had been educated under communism.

Neither I nor my team of expert advisors are Luddites. We have much respect and appreciation for cyber inventions and the science behind them, even AI. However, we all share the concern of many in the scientific community and beyond regarding the moral, ethical, and even spiritual implications of the rapidly developing technology.

This, then, is a book focused on the largest of concerns about the rapidly developing phenomena of artificial intelligence. The message here is an alert to everyone and a special appeal for the wisdom of "scientists with a conscience." Chris Matyszczyk is among those who see some of the deeper issues we must face. "The rise of the authoritarian machine seems 'not too distant,'" says Matyszczyk in writing about Levandowski's vision.[34] There is really no way to keep this from happening, says Levandowski, so we need to give up trying. In fact, "This feeling of *we must stop this* is rooted in twenty-first century anthropomorphism."

Chris Matyszczyk raises an important concern, "But doesn't anthropomorphism mean applying human characteristics to non-humans and objects?" This is the core issue of this book. As we present in a coming chapter, human beings are *Imago Dei,* made in the image of God, but the AI machines are *imago hominis,* built in the image of the human, who, according to the Bible, "falls short" of the glorious character of God because of the entry of evil (Romans 3:23).

The ancient problem of humanity's fall into sin is thus the major driver of angst in the age of artificial intelligence. "AI

---

[34] "The new Church of the AI God is even creepier than I imagined," By Chris Matyszczyk, *c/net.*, November 16, 2017. Retrieved from https://www.cnet.com/news/the-new-church-of-ai-god-is-even-creepier-than-i-imagined/, July 21, 2018.

is only as good as those who create it," says John Curry, a member of my team of expert advisors on this book.

This is the core concern we address in these pages and the cause of the concern felt by many who are thinking through the implications of the rising dominance of artificial intelligence.

CHAPTER 1

Einstein and the Angst
of the Titans

*The computer programmer is a creator of universes
for which he alone is the lawgiver.*
—Joseph Weizenbaum[35]

David Rothman did a double take when he spotted the famous man who had ambled into his store in Peconic, New York, on that day in June 1939.

Albert Einstein was walking up and down the aisles of Rothman's Department Store out on Nassau Point. Rothman wondered for a moment how he ought to treat the titan of science. He decided to handle Einstein as he would any other shopper.

"Are you looking for something in particular?" Rothman asked.

---

[35] As cited in Ray Kurzweil, *The Age of Spiritual Machines: When Computers Exceed Human Intelligence* (New York: Penguin Books, 1999) Kindle loc. 1630 of 9961.

"Sundials," Einstein responded with a guttural German intonation.

"I do have one in my backyard," Rothman replied.

Einstein laughed as he pointed to his feet. He had asked for "sandals," but his German accent spun out "sundials."

As Einstein was at the counter paying for his sandals, he heard classical music flowing from a phonograph. Einstein and Rothman began talking about a shared appreciation for the classics, and Rothman told the eminent scientist that he was a violinist.

Einstein was excited to hear that because he too was a violinist. "We must play together some time," he said.

A few days later, Rothman appeared at Einstein's rental house with his violin. Einstein was delighted to see him. The renowned physicist suggested they play a piece from Bach that Einstein had selected. It quickly became apparent that Rothman couldn't keep up with Einstein.

"Let's talk instead," said Einstein, as he laid down his violin.

Rothman had only an elementary-grade education but was passionate about philosophy and science. He might not be able to hold his own with Einstein in playing the violin, and by no means was he the scientist's equal in physics. Nevertheless, the storekeeper and the titan of physics sat on Einstein's front porch conversing on their shared favorite topics for a long time.

Hours later, Einstein's housekeeper suddenly appeared and wagged her finger at Rothman. "You are keeping Dr. Einstein awake!" she said.

"No, I am keeping Mr. Rothman awake!" Einstein instantly replied.

The two men wound up spending a lot of time together that summer on Einstein's porch, mostly talking about science. At their last session in 1946, Einstein told Rothman, "I have had the most wonderful summer of my entire life, and this I owe to your initiative."[36]

But there was another day in 1939 when Einstein had different visitors who had also come to his summer cottage to discuss science. The outcome of that conversation would change history.

Leo Szilard, a Hungarian physicist known to Einstein and also living in the United States, had growing concern about what he was hearing regarding nuclear fission. Niels Bohr, a Danish scientist, spoke at the Fifth Washington Conference in Theoretical Physics on January 26, 1939, and Szilard began to contemplate what Bohr was reporting. He realized that what Bohr was describing—and a large swath of the physics community was abuzz about—could ultimately lead to the release of a vast amount of atomic energy in the form of a bomb. Enrico Fermi and John R. Dunning would soon perform experiments that supported the claims.

Szilard thought of Hitler and the tensions building in Europe under the rise of the Nazis. He knew it would be only a matter of time until German scientists would also be experimenting with nuclear fission. Szilard urgently felt that American President Franklin D. Roosevelt must be informed of the developments.

---

[36] "Einstein and My Grandfather," By Chuck Rothman. Retrieved from https://sites.google.com/site/chuckrothmansf/einstein, January 2, 2018.

But who had the clout to get the president's attention? *Einstein*, Szilard suddenly realized.

So, on July 12, 1939, the same summer Einstein was enjoying his chats with David Rothman, Leo Szilard and another Hungarian physicist, Eugene Wigner, came motoring up the driveway at Einstein's rented retreat. They persuaded Einstein to write the president.

In the letter written August 2, 1939, Einstein told Roosevelt:

> Some recent work by Fermi and L. Szilard, which has been communicated to me in manuscript, leads me to expect that the element uranium may be turned into a new and important source of energy in the immediate future. [...] Certain aspects of the situation which has arisen seem to call for watchfulness and, if necessary, quick action on the part of the Administration. [...] This new phenomenon would also lead to the construction of bombs, and it is conceivable—though much less certain—that extremely powerful bombs of a new type may thus be constructed.

Einstein, Szilard, and Wigner, with others in the scientific community who were concerned about the implications of nuclear power, came to be called "scientists with a conscience." That distinguished them from scientists who were so hypnotized by their discoveries that they never thought through the consequences for individuals and humanity itself.

As artificial intelligence grows more dominant and invasive, there is an urgent need for "scientists with a conscience" now. The titans today are those who dominate the information-science-technology sector. And some of them are very anxious and showing themselves to have a strong sense of conscience.

"The rise of AI could be the worst or the best thing that has happened for humanity," warned Stephen Hawking.[37]

Even some of the "Masters of the Universe" who lead giant enterprises creating mind-numbing applications of computer science are concerned. Elon Musk frets that "with artificial intelligence we are summoning the demon."[38] He is concerned about "deep intelligence" in the network, and where that might lead.

Musk has expressed a major nightmare for some of the titans of Silicon Valley[39]—the ability of AI machines to enlarge their knowledge and develop networks of deep intelligence beyond human capacities or awareness. "Once humans develop artificial intelligence, it would take off on its own, and redesign itself at an ever-increasing rate," said Stephen Hawking in 2014. "Humans, who are limited by slow biological evolution, couldn't compete and would be superseded."[40]

This could lead to a complex of machines sharing such information and comprising a silicon-based cybersphere in direct competition with the creators in the carbon-based biosphere. Might that super-intelligence at some point recognize what many contemporary humans don't—the flawed nature of

---

[37] "Stephen Hawking Issues Stern Warning on AI: Could Be 'Worst Thing' for Humanity," By John Koetsier, *Forbes.com,* November 6, 2017. Retrieved from https://www.forbes.com/sites/johnkoetsier/2017/11/06/stephen-hawking-is-sues-stern-warning-on-ai-could-be-worst-thing-for-humanity/#1991e4953a7c, July 21, 2018.

[38] Retrieved from https://techcrunch.com/2014/10/26/elon-musk-com-pares-building-artificial-intelligence-to-summoning-the-demon/, June 6, 2018.

[39] "Silicon Valley" as used in this book is a symbol for the cyber-industry glob-ally, and not just the area of California bearing that name.

[40] "Stephen Hawking warns artificial intelligence could end mankind," By Rory Cellan-Jones, bbc.com, December 2, 2014. Retrieved from https://www.bbc.com/news/technology-30290540.

human beings—and conclude that humanity is a threat that must be eliminated?

"Artificial intelligence is a fundamental risk to human civilization," said Musk.

He is not alone in his concerns. Dr. Ryan Calo has called for a Federal Robotics Commission because AI robots "make possible new human experiences and create distinct but related challenges that would benefit from being examined and treated together."[41]

The "new human experiences" and "distinct but related challenges" are among the goblins that keep some scientists awake at night. The angst is so widespread that at this writing, more than 8,000 signatures, including those of Hawking and Musk, were attached to an open letter reminiscent of Einstein's epistle to Franklin Roosevelt.

The style of the "open letter" is, like Einstein's, without hysteria, but the angst is there in its concerns and appeals, as excerpts show:

> Artificial intelligence (AI) research has explored a variety of problems and approaches since its inception, but for the last 20 years or so has been focused on the problems surrounding the construction of intelligent agents—systems that perceive and act in some environment. [...] There is now a broad consensus that AI research is progressing steadily, and that its impact on society is likely to increase. The potential benefits are huge, since everything that civilization has to

---

[41] "The case for a federal robotics commission," By Ryan Calo, September 15, 2014. Retrieved from https://www.brookings.edu/research/the-case-for-a-federal-robotics-commission/.

offer is a product of human intelligence; we cannot predict what we might achieve when this intelligence is magnified by the tools AI may provide, but the eradication of disease and poverty are not unfathomable. Because of the great potential of AI, it is important to research how to reap its benefits while avoiding potential pitfalls. [...] We recommend expanded research aimed at ensuring that increasingly capable AI systems are robust and beneficial: our AI systems must do what we want them to do.[42]

The experts and scholars are seeing the extremes to which AI can lead. Though the scientific mavens might not agree—and if so, this is a big hole in their thinking—the extremes will come from human beings totally cut off from God and His Transcendent Holiness and Being.

Yet humanity has a hard time suppressing the hunger for transcendence. Thus, an Anthony Levandowski rushes to proclaim the new god and get a church going to spread the new gospel.

Our contention in this book is that it is not so much the machines about which we should be concerned, but the people, their worldviews and moral and ethical values, and especially spiritual principles that they bring to their work. That will determine whether AI will be a blessing or curse on humanity. Calo's concern in proposing the Federal Robotics Commission is the possibility of irresponsible innovation.

Some critics of people seeking to live by the biblical worldview and work hard to minister its truth say they are not

---

[42] An Open Letter: Research Priorities for Robust and Beneficial Artificial Intelligence," *Future of Life Institute.* Retrieved from https://futureoflife.org/ ai-open-letter/?cn-reloaded=1, July 21, 2018.

living in the real world. The truth is that individuals who reject Romans 3:23 which says that "all have sinned and come short of the glory of God" are living in an illusory world. The real world faces the fact of sin, its consequences, and the need for a solution.

Yet, though sin has caused humans to fall from God's glorious character, man and woman were made in the image of God. Our universal recognition of good and evil is evidence that we know something is wrong, that there is misalignment between human behavior and higher standards. If we reject the belief in the transcendent, what then will we build into the robots?

All that is left is our fallenness.

The machine may expand its own quantitative capacities to a level far exceeding that of its human makers, but what will be its qualitative values?

The bottom line is the question of transcendence—what provides ultimate value and a point of accountability for the AI builders? What is the highest standard by which they define themselves and their behavioral choices? *Who or what will be regarded as transcendent authority in the mind of artificial intelligence?*

This is at the core of the crisis of artificial intelligence and transcendence in our age.

CHAPTER 2

The Life-Death Importance of True Transcendence

It must be of the spirit if we are to save the flesh.
—Douglas MacArthur

I was born December 5, 1941, two days before the Japanese attack on Pearl Harbor that brought the United States into the Second World War. My childhood was filled with the scratchy newsreel images of the battles and giant personalities of the era.

One of my earliest memories was hanging out the window of our family car as we drove slowly through the streets of our city in an impromptu parade celebrating the end of the war. Thus, many years later, I could hardly believe that I was shaking the hand of Mitsuo Fuchida, the Japanese pilot who had led the attack on Pearl Harbor. Even more astonishing, I met Fuchida at an American church where he had just preached.

After the war, Fuchida became a Christian and then an evangelist, proclaiming the Gospel throughout Japan and the world—including the United States upon whose territory he had led the attack years earlier. Fuchida gave his life to Christ after reading a tract by a former American POW in Japan, Jacob DeShazer, who had returned to Japan as a missionary.

DeShazer would not have been there had it not been for the American general who was hailed as Japan's conqueror but who also opened the way for the Christian Gospel to enter Japanese society.[43]

General Douglas MacArthur faced immense challenges when he was assigned to help the Japanese rebuild their nation following the devastation of the Second World War. The country's national pride was broken, and their government was in shambles, their economy shattered, their educational system in ruins, and their politics in a state of upheaval after its defeat. Japan had also been the target for the first use of the atomic bomb. The terrifying weapon about which Einstein had warned President Franklin Roosevelt had become shocking reality to the world as the cities of Hiroshima and Nagasaki were leveled in the blasts.

As Supreme Commander for the Allied Powers in Japan, MacArthur had been given sweeping powers to reconstruct the society and its infrastructure. The General may not have been a theologian, but he read his Bible daily, carrying it with him everywhere he went. Though he may not have known the details of the doctrine of transcendence, MacArthur intuitively sought to set its principles at the core of the new Japan.

MacArthur felt that "the problem" with the human race and wars "basically is theological and involves a spiritual recrudescence and improvement of human character that will synchronize with our almost matchless advances in science,

---

[43] The story is powerfully told by T. Martin Bennett in *Wounded Tiger* (Dallas: Brown Books Publishing House, 2016)

art, literature and all material and cultural developments of the last two thousand years. It must be of the spirit if we are to save the flesh."[44]

MacArthur understood that Japan, prior to and during World War II, was a theocracy, with the emperor, who was viewed as divine, at the center. MacArthur did not want the nation to continue with theocratic rule and persuaded Emperor Hirohito to deny his divinity. Rather than a forced religion, the new Japan would have freedom of belief and worship.

Nevertheless, MacArthur believed Christianity to be the answer for the Japanese. "I asked for missionaries and more missionaries," he wrote in his memoir, *Reminiscences.* "Whenever possible I told visiting ministers of the need for their work in Japan," he said. "The more missionaries we can bring out here, and the more occupation troops we can send home, the better."[45] At MacArthur's request, the Pocket Testament League provided ten million Bibles in the Japanese language.

MacArthur has been criticized by some historians. Perhaps his use of religion was strictly utilitarian. However, his own convictions were that the right spirituality is essential for improvement of human character. It would be the organizing center for all human endeavors that would provide the order and peace that heal fragmentation and conflict.

What Japan needed in 1945 in the aftermath of war is what many others believe all the nations need now in all of their institutions, especially the Big Five that define and propagate cultural consensus: the Information Establishment,

---

[44] MacArthur's Farewell Speech to Congress, 1951.
[45] Around The World In 80 Days, Day 15: Japan, A Post-War Miracle And Model | The Daily Caller

Entertainment Establishment, Academic Establishment, Political Establishment, and Corporate Establishment. For example, Professor Luigi Zingales of the University of Chicago believes that Big Tech expansion poses "a threat ... to the function of our democracy." Zingales points out that:

> Google and Facebook know more about us than our spouses or closest friends—and sometimes even more than we know about ourselves. They can predict what we are going to do, how we're going to vote, and what products we are going to buy. And they use the best minds to manipulate our decisions.[46]

Zingales' concern was for regulation that would prevent the incursion of AI and other technologies into our personal lives and freedoms. That issue is much larger than the mere need for governmental laws constraining technology. It brings the broader realization that *something regarded as ultimate must limit those who would grab for total power over us*. It will either be True Transcendence, the recognition of God's authority, or regulation and law, the imposition of human power.

"A culture that does not aspire to the divine becomes obsessed with the fascination of evil, reveling in the frivolous, the depraved, and the bestial," says economist and AI expert George Gilder.[47] What we regard as ultimate authority—transcendence—is truly a matter of life and death. We must have True Transcendence if we are to be free and secure in our liberties.

---

[46] Should We Regulate Big Tech?", by Luigi Zingales (*Imprimis: A Publication of Hillsdale College,* November 2018, Vol.47, No.11), 3.
[47] Glenn H. Utter, *Culture Wars in America: A Documentary and Reference Guide* (Greenwood, 2009), 73.

In the absence of a transcendent view, many have knowingly or unknowingly adopted the religion of humanitarianism in which the human is "the measure of all things," according to Daniel J. Mahoney, who sees this as the "central heresy" in our time. "Humanitarianism apart from a transcendent moral order quickly becomes 'anti-human in decisive respects,'" writes reviewer David P. Deaval, quoting Mahoney.[48]

To deny that the human has a spiritual and political nature is an "ideological lie" of "protean character," thinks Mahoney. Without *the* moral law, human beings will invent a moral law, albeit one that is arbitrary, confused, and confusing, even to its enforcers," writes Deaval in his review.[49] Is this the moral and ethical confusion being programmed into artificial intelligence? Mahoney understands conscience as the "cognitive and moral order that transcends mere subjectivity." True conscience is a matter of the spirit. *Where, then, is the locus of conscience in the machine?*

Further, there are many claims to transcendence from the worship of gods to the acknowledgement of the divine right of kings. How do we distinguish True Transcendence from all the claimants and pretenders? Here are some (among many) of the distinguishing marks delineating True Transcendence from the counterfeit varieties:

- True Transcendence is *the* Singularity, while counterfeit transcendence is mere uniqueness.

---

[48] "Our Spiritual Opioid Crisis," by David P. Deaval, *National Review,* January 10, 2019. Retrieved from https://www.nationalreview.com/magazine/2019/01/28/the-idol-of-our-age-book-review/, January 25, 2019.
[49] Daniel J. Mahoney's book is *The Idol of Our Age: How the Religion of Humanity Subverts Christianity* (Encounter Books, 2018).

A genuine Singularity is not merely unique because uniqueness is a classification made in the comparisons and contrasts
between objects. True Transcendence is *incomparable,* not an
object whose worth is to be evaluated by comparison to other
objects. This is among the reasons idolatry is an abomination.
If deity is a statue, competing religionists can compare and
contrast and argue that their idol is prettier, scarier, or more
glorious than another. True Transcendence is spirit with
Being beyond all that exists, and True Transcendence does
not exist as one among many or several. True Transcendence
may give rise to others in its image, but it will not be dimin-
ished by what comes from it. God creates and procreates but
is not lessened in His Being and majesty or outranked by
His progeny. To worship the universe or any object within
it, including humans and other life-forms, is idolatry because
the universe is not transcendent.

This is illustrated in Jesus of Nazareth. Though in His non-in-
carnate state He is all that God is and therefore truly transcendent (Hebrews 1:1-3), in His incarnation, He sets aside
the prerogatives of Deity (Philippians 2). Jesus of Nazareth,
in His incarnation, is indeed singular among human beings.
He is *Christ, the* "Anointed of God," clothed in the flesh of
humanity so He can represent humanity in His Atonement for
humanity. He is also the "only begotten" of God (John 3:16),
indicating Jesus Christ is the only One among all humanity to
be the direct offspring of God the Father (Luke 2).

Humans are thus made to desire and recognize transcendence.
To paraphrase Augustine, the human heart was made by God
for God, and only God can fill it. When we ignore or forget
the biblical revelation and its implications, we try to create our
own transcendent objects and beings. Artificial intelligence is
perhaps the end of humanity's search for "Singularity."

About artificial intelligence, the "technological singularity" will be reached by 2045, predicts futurologist Ray Kurzweil. By 2029, he believes artificial intelligence will pass the Turing Test and will have "human level intelligence." The "Singularity" occurs as AI machines are smarter than human brains. "That leads to computers having human intelligence, our putting them inside our brains, connecting them to the cloud," expanding who we are," says Kurzweil. He notes that this is not merely "a future scenario," but one that is already here "in part, and it's going to accelerate."[50]

While the AI machine may go beyond human intelligence and therefore be admired and even worshipped as transcendent, it will only be so on a relative scale. As discussed above, God alone is transcendent in the Absolute, and this is the primary determinant between True Transcendence and its counterfeit.

God's singular Being is implicit in the name by which He identifies Himself at the request of Moses before the burning bush: *I Am.* God alone dwells in perpetual "am-ness." All others are locked in finite time. They must have a "birth day" and will most certainly have a "death day."

Recorded in 1 Samuel 2, "Hannah's Song of Thanksgiving" expresses the singular nature of God—along with other Scriptures. The mother of the great prophet Samuel sings:

---

[50] "Kurzweil Claims That the Singularity Will Happen by 2045," by Christianna Reedy, futurism.com, October 5, 2017. Retrieved from https://futurism.com/kurzweil-claims-that-the-singularity-will-happen-by-2045, December 7, 2018.

There is no one holy like the Lord,
Indeed, there is no one besides You,
Nor is there any rock like our God.

(1 Samuel 2:2, NIV)

King David recognizes God's Singularity when he prays in 1 Chronicles 17:20, "O Lord, there is none like You, nor is there any God besides You." In Psalms 86:8, David prays,

There is no one like You among the gods, O Lord,
Nor are there any works like Yours.

The same understanding is present in David's son Solomon at the dedication of the great Temple he builds for the manifest presence of God and His worship. Solomon prays that "all the peoples of the earth may know that the Lord is God; *there is no one else*" (1 Kings 8:60, italics added).

Singularity also means non-contingency. The AI god is contingent on its builder and the information programmed into its circuits. The True Transcendent is, as we suggest elsewhere, contingent on nothing for His Being. The only necessity for His existence is within Himself. Thus, God is, as Thomas Aquinas wrote, *ipsum esse subsistens*—God is absolute Being, therefore making it possible for all that exists to exist.

This is among the greatest errors of idolatry. Idols are made by human hands or human declaration, but God exists in and of Himself, as we have noted in the discussion about *aseity* (self-generating its own being and existence). There we concluded that one must either believe in the aseity of the *Creator* God or the aseity of the *created* universe (a contradiction). However, science itself has shown that the cosmos does not possess the attribute of aseity, for there is an event that brings it into existence.

Futurist George Gilder writes,

> "Let there be light," says the Bible. All the firmaments of technology, all our computers and networks, are built with light, and of light, and for light, to hasten its spread around the world. [...] From Newton, Maxwell, and Einstein to Richard Feynman to Charles Townes, the more men have gazed at light, the more it turns out to be a phenomenon utterly different from anything else. And yet everything else—every atom and every molecule—is fraught with oscillating intensity.[51]

- True Transcendence is complete and not in process, but counterfeit transcendence must *acquire* and is therefore always in a developmental process.

The biggest clue that the coming AI god is not truly transcendent is in the statement of AI church founder Anthony Levandowski that the artificial intelligence that "is going to be created will effectively be a god."

Anything that must be created or developed cannot be truly transcendent. Process is relevant only in the context of *kronos,* finite time. Such time comes into existence at the point of creation. But as we explore in Chapter Five, there is reality that must precede creation, or nothing that came into being could have come into being, to paraphrase John 1:1. God exists in *kairos,* an eternal state of being, outside of the tensed time of *kronos;* therefore, it is meaningless to speak of creating God or of something becoming God.

---

[51] George Gilder, *Telecosm: How Infinite Bandwidth Will Revolutionize Our World* (Free Press, 200), 31.

Both the Old and New Testaments have much to say about the *immutability* of God. "God is not a man, that He should lie, nor a son of man, that He should repent" (Numbers 23:19). God Himself attests that "I, the Lord, do not change" (Malachi 3:6). The New Testament bears witness to the same reality. Jesus Christ, Hebrews 1:3 reveals, "is the radiance" of God's glory and the exact representation of His nature. Hebrews 13:8 then says, "Jesus Christ is the same, yesterday and today and forever." Further, God is "the Father of Lights, with whom there is no variation or shifting shadow" (James 1:17).

"God is unchanging in His being, perfections, purposes, and promises, yet God does act and feel emotions, and He acts and feels differently in response to different situations," writes theologian Wayne Grudem.[52]

- True Transcendence is mystery that is revealed, but counterfeit transcendence is illusion that is contrived.

The Bible speaks of the "mystery" of God in His majestic transcendence. One of Job's friends asks:

> Can you discover the depths of God?
> Can you discover the limits of the Almighty?
> They are high as the heavens, what can you do?
> Deeper than Sheol, what can you know?
>
> (Job 11:7-9)

"Great is the mystery of godliness," writes Paul in in 1 Timothy 3:16. In 1 Corinthians 2:7, the Apostle speaks of "the wisdom of God" as "mystery, hidden wisdom which God ordained before the ages for our glory." In the *Apocalypse,* the

---

[52] Wayne Grudem, *Systematic Theology: An Introduction to Bible Doctrine* (Leicester, England: Inter-Varsity Press; Grand Rapids: Zondervan Publishing House, 1994) 163.

Revelation vision, John sees a time coming when "the mystery of God would be finished" (Revelation 17:5).

All this is an affront to secularized humanity.

"A mystery goes *beyond reason* but not *against reason,*" writes Norman Geisler.[53] Human hubris is insulted by the notion of ultimate mystery, that anything could exist beyond human rational discovery and understanding. Pride demands an answer, for no iota of fact to be beyond its understanding. The human who was made in the image of God, the image that sin marred and the prideful human resists, nevertheless people want the attributes of God, among which is omniscience. Men and women love to toy with mystery as entertainment, but at the end of the day—or the final commercial break— they presume that they will be able to solve all mysteries.

We might even go so far to say that mystery is an offense to the secular technological mind. The resistance against transcendence and its fade are part of the "disenchantment" Charles Taylor writes about in *The Secular Age.*[54] Taylor describes three features of the worldview that "made the presence of God seemingly undeniable" to pre-secularized humanity: (1) "The natural world they lived in, which had its place in the cosmos they imagined, testified to divine purpose and action..."; (2) "God was also implicated in the very existence of society. [...] A kingdom could only be conceived as grounded in something higher than mere human action in secular time"; (3) "People lived in an 'enchanted' world [...] the world of spirits, demons, and moral forces."[55]

---

[53] Norman Geisler, *The Baker Encyclopedia of Apologetics* (Grand Rapids: Baker Publishing, date??), 515
[54] Charles Taylor, *A Secular Age* (Harvard University Press, 2018).
[55] Charles Taylor, *A Secular Age* (Cambridge and London: The Belknap Press of Harvard University Press, 2007), 25-26.

Disenchantment strips away all of these worldview components, and all we are left with is the technological and mechanical. A thoroughly mechanistic mentality seeks to deconstruct and deny (or explain away) mystery.

This is part of the great drive to produce artificial intelligence that will answer all questions. Such inventive people dream of the day that goes beyond the era of *Alexa* and *Siri,* when the "ask" command unveils more than a faster driving route or nearest Mexican restaurant, but the very secrets of the universe itself. The arrogant presumption is that it is the right of man to know all things, and the universe itself is answerable if it refuses to yield its secrets and reveal what's behind its mysteries.

The human in the desperation to vie with True Transcendence and achieve omniscience will finally create illusion, Wizard of Oz contraptions, to imitate magic and the deeper knowledge (*gnosis*) presumably underlying it. On a more mundane level, therefore, Orwell's Big Brother speaks in a smarmy, seemingly caring voice, trying to give Winston Smith, Orwell's protagonist, the illusion that Big Brother's austere requirements arise from a caring heart. There is no heart there, however, just circuits under the control of a tyrannical elite that demands conformity to its rules or suffer the consequences.

Hardly any events illustrate the illusionary contrivance better than an event that happened in Russia at a technology conference. "A robot hailed in Russia as the latest in cutting-edge technology has been unmasked—as a man in a suit," reported Florence Snead, on December 13, 2018. Observers noted movements that were too human-like, plus there seemed to be human skin just visible in a crease in the $4,000 robot suit's neck. The company that made the robotic outfit boasted that it could create an "almost complete illusion that you have a real robot." [56]

- True Transcendence is greatly revered, but counterfeit transcendence is merely regarded.

Revering God is often spoken of in the Bible as "fearing" God. The fear of God is the beginning of wisdom.[57] This is so because the wise person knows that God requires accountability for human actions.

In *The Devil's Delusion,* David Berlinski tells of an encounter between a Nazi SS officer and a Jewish man in an East European village at the beginning of Hitler's invasions in the East. The officer stood holding his machine gun as he ordered the old man to dig his own grave. "God is watching what you are doing," the elderly Hasidic Jew said. And with that, the Nazi soldier shot him.

Berlinski, reflecting on God's transcendence and the accountability it infers, wrote,

> What Hitler did *not* believe and what Stalin did *not* believe and what Mao did *not* believe and what the SS did *not* believe and what the Gestapo did *not* believe and what the NKVD did *not* believe and what the commissars, functionaries, swaggering executioners, Nazi doctors, Communist Party theoreticians [...] and a thousand party hacks did *not* believe was that God was watching what they were doing.[58]

---

[56] https://inews.co.uk/news/technology/russian-robot-boris-man-in-suit-russia-24/

[57] Proverbs 9:10, *et al.*

[58] David Berlinksi, *The Devil's Delusion: Atheism and its Scientific Pretensions* (New York: Basic Books, 2009), 26.

The inescapable implication is this: *a human being never has to fear another human being who fears the holy, loving, transcendent God.*

This fear of God in His transcendent holiness was on Thomas Jefferson's mind when he wrote his *Notes on the State of Virginia* in 1781. Jefferson reflects on the nature and source of freedom and rhetorically asks, "And can the liberties of a nation be thought secure when we have removed their only firm basis, a conviction in the minds of the people that these liberties are of the gift of God? That they are not to be violated but with his wrath?"

Jefferson recognizes that there are many human beings in America who are not free but in slavery and that he himself is a slaveholder. He writes,

> Indeed, I tremble for my country when I reflect that God is just: that his justice cannot sleep for ever: that considering numbers, nature, and natural means only, a revolution of the wheel of fortune, an exchange of situation, is among possible events: that it may become probable by supernatural interference! The Almighty has no attribute which can take side with us in such a contest.

Sadly, Jefferson, Washington, and other American founders who held slaves felt that abolition was too complex an issue to address at that point. They kicked the can down the road for future generations. The justice of the transcendent God did not stay asleep, and in 1860, America tore itself apart with brother killing brother. Even in the twenty-first century, the nation bears the judgment socially, politically, and culturally.

Counterfeit transcendence is without a sense of accountability to a Supreme Being who is holy and just. The justice of God is as much an attribute of Deity as mercy. Therefore, it is inevitable that the justice of God will demand an account and render the consequences of injustice. The Kingdom of God is characterized by justice as much as peace and joy (Romans 14:17).

Therefore, if AI is god, what transcendent boundaries will govern the machine's interactions with human beings (until we reach Ray Kurzweil's golden age in which we all become machines)? What is the algorithm that establishes true justice as defined by the perfections of God?

The great terror in Orwell's *Nineteen Eighty-Four* was the continual, probing stare of Big Brother. There was no fear of God in the machine. Therefore, all on whom it looked trembled in the presence of those cold mechanical eyes. No grace, no mercy—just the relentless, judgmental robotic probe.

What a contrast to the eyes of the true and living God!

True, God's eyes "are in every place, keeping watch on the evil and the good" (Proverbs 15:3). But these are the eyes of the *Father*, not an uncaring tyrant or AI robotic image. He is watching as a daddy watches for the bad things that will harm his child. That also means observing for the destructive things in the child's life that might hurt or destroy the little one. "I will counsel you with my eye upon you," the Father says (Psalm 32:8, ESV).

Therefore, "The eyes of the Lord move to and fro throughout the earth that He may strongly support those who hearts are completely His" (2 Chronicles 16:9).

The hard fact is that we will have upon us either the eyes of the loving Father or the stare of the indifferent machines and their apathetic algorithms.

People in "Oceania," Orwell's fictitious world, had no choice but to regard the presence of the electronic eyes with fear. However, those who truly fear God do so as His children. They trust Him as loving. They know God the Father disciplines them, but He does so as *Abba,* not as a cold, merciless mechanism pretending to be human. Those who know Him and who open their lives to His love exult in living *Coram Deo*—before the face of God (Hebrews 12:5-6).

No man-made object possesses True Transcendence. Machines can frighten us and even control us, but it's not because we *revere* them. It's because we have no choice but to *regard* their existence and position with respect to our lives and choices.

- True Transcendence has eternal Being, but counterfeit transcendence has temporal existence.

Science, especially since Newton and Einstein, speaks of different time coordinates. One is absolute time, the temporal occurrence of events throughout the universe. The other is relative time, that which we experience in the events of our lives that move from past and present into the future.

The Bible also reveals time on two levels, as we have discussed elsewhere. *Kairos* brings fulfillment of purpose into *kronos.* The Bible speaks of this reality as the "fullness of time" (e.g., Galatians 4). Time is not an apt word for *kairos* because time infers limited duration. *Kairos* is the content of which *kronos* is the vessel. Yet because *Kairos* has reality that is manifested on the *kronos* scale, it is thought of as a type of time and translated as such in scriptural passages.

True Transcendence is beyond finite *kronos* time but can engage with it. William Lane Craig writes that "God transcends time altogether."[59] Craig says,

> Given His permanent, beginningless and endless existence, God must be omnitemporal. [...] He exists at every moment of time there ever is. I do not mean that He exists at every time at once. [...] He existed at every past moment, He exists at the present moment, and He will exist at every future moment.[60]

But the best of machinery is caught in the laws of finite time. Parts deteriorate and must be replaced. Even if a machine can replicate its parts and repair itself, that does not mean it has escaped finitude for the very need for repair, replacement, and improvement is a testimony to the finitude of the machine.

Thus, far from being cast aside on the trash heap of exhausted esoterica, depleted delusions, failed fantasies, and silly spiritualisms, the belief in True Transcendence is of immense practical importance.

This becomes clear as we look at some of the effects of True Transcendence on our personal lives, institutions, nations, and civilizations, all the way to the world itself.

---

[59] William Lane Craig, *Time and Eternity*, 29.
[60] Craig, 15.

CHAPTER 3

The Effects of True Transcendence

Genesis is ... claiming that ethics is not relativistic, nor did it evolve horizontally through some evolutionary processes ... but it was transcendent in its origin. Part of the image of God is seen in the fact that humans are moral beings.

—John Lennox[61]

As described in the Foreword, Otis Graf was a young aerospace engineer working at NASA's Johnson Space Center when on Christmas Eve in 1968, the sense of transcendence suddenly broke through in Mission Control and for many across the world. He remembers the stunning moment when Astronaut Frank Borman, aboard the spacecraft approaching the moon, read from the Bible, Genesis 1.

Graf had just spent two years working for the Peace Corps in the jungles of southeast Asia, touching the world's need and pain. And as 1968 ended, he was looking far beyond those jungles into the heavens.

---

[61] John Lennox, *2084: Artificial Intelligence and the Future of Humanity* (Grand Rapids: Zondervan Reflective, 2020), 141.

Graf's interest in space travel had been ignited in 1957 with the Soviet Union's launch of Sputnik into earth-orbit. Five years later, he was reflecting on the words of Soviet cosmonauts Yuri Gagarin and Gherman Titov, respectively, the first and second humans in space who were put there by an atheistic state. Gagarin told the world he had seen neither "God nor angels" there. Later, Titov proclaimed that "no God" had built the rockets that propelled them into orbit. "I do not believe in god. [...] I believe in man, his strength, his possibilities and his reason," said Titov.

For young Otis Graf, the statements of the Soviet cosmonauts went far beyond theology. "During that time, any thoughtful person could imagine the enormous impact of a Soviet cosmonaut circling or being the first to walk on the moon," Graf remembers. It would seem to signal the superiority of an entire belief system, including Communism and atheism.

Then came the remarkable breakthrough of transcendence on December 24, 1968.

The eyes of America and much of the world were on the social and political chaos in the United States. Racial riots, the violence in Chicago during the national convention of the Democrats, and the assassination of Dr. Martin Luther King along with massive protests against United States involvement in Vietnam riveted the focus of multitudes on the earth and its problems.

Then Frank Borman turned the attention of many to the heavens as he read God's words recorded in the Bible's first chapter.

In his book, *Rocket Men,* Robert Kurson described what happened in Mission Control and NASA's Houston complex—and beyond:

> Inside Mission Control, no one moved. Then, one after another, these scientists and engineers in Houston began to cry. The agency had allowed the crew to choose what to say to the world on Christmas Eve. [...] It had come as a complete surprise to them. In his studio at CBS, Walter Cronkite fought back tears as he came back on air. [...] Watching in Houston, Susan Borman wept.[62]

A half-century later, Otis Graf says he believes the long-term accomplishment of Borman's Christmas message was that, once and for all, it defeated political propaganda and aggressive national aspirations as a reason for putting people and equipment into space. International cooperation in space became the norm and replaced struggles between competing ideologies.

This was an effect of that moment when the world, for a brief span of time, focused on God's majestic transcendence.

Seven years earlier, President Dwight Eisenhower was contemplating the *immanent* scale and was anxious. Eisenhower expressed two concerns about the future as his presidency drew to a close in 1961. On one hand, he warned about the growth of the "military-industrial complex," and on the other, he warned about the "scientific-technological elite."

Eisenhower may not have understood how prophetic he was. The grave threat to humanity now is the "scientific-

---

[62] Rocket men: Inside story of first astronauts to orbit the moon - NZ Herald

technological elite" developing their projects, including and especially artificial intelligence, without any sense of True Transcendence, and in some cases, outright defiance of God Himself.

Eisenhower's words in 1961 are strikingly prescient and relevant for the age of AI. The "sweeping changes in our industrial-military posture ... has been the technological revolution during recent decades," he said. "Today, the solitary inventor, tinkering in his shop, has been overshadowed by task forces in laboratories and retesting fields." Universities had become dependent on federal funds as they broadened their research programs. "(T)he power of money is ever present—and is gravely to be regarded," said President Eisenhower, adding, *"For every blackboard there are now hundreds of new electronic computers"* (italics added).

But Eisenhower saw something else. Because of the huge costs to do scientific research and the need for government funds, "We should also be alert to the equal and opposite danger that public policy could itself become the captive of a scientific-technological elite."

Scientific advance is important to the well-being of humanity, including the development of artificial intelligence to serve but not suppress us. How do we go forward with needed technologies without destroying ourselves in the process?

The answer is to recognize our capacities to think and produce as the gift of God and our accountability to Him for our work. "Whatever you do in word or deed, do all to the glory of God," writes Paul in 1 Corinthians 10:31. If we do that, we have nothing to fear. To ignore True Transcendence is to push forward into a grim and dangerous future.

The peril is implied in contemporary times and the loss of the sense of transcendence in concerns raised by Yuval Harari:

> We have advanced from canoes to galleys to steam ships to space shuttles—but nobody knows where we are going. [...] Self-made gods with only the laws of physics to keep us company, we are accountable to no one. [...] *Is there anything more dangerous than dissatisfied and irresponsible gods who don't know what they want?*[63]

In Chapter 2, we contrasted True Transcendence with counterfeit versions. As we explore here some of the practical outcomes of living and working under True Transcendence, we see how blessings can come to society through science and technology pursued *Coram Deo*—before the Face of God who is perfect in His character, glorious in His Being, and awesome in the equilibrium of His love and justice.

- True Transcendence has a transformative effect.

What provides your *lift?*

This is a vital question that goes to the heart of passion, motive, and intent. The "world, the flesh, and the devil" all exert a powerful pull downward on human nature. As we discuss in another chapter, spiritual, moral, and mental "gravity" continually tug on us. The Apostle Paul aspired to the highest but struggled with the constant push to the lowest. He spoke for us all—whether we acknowledge it or not—when he cried, "What I am doing I do not understand; for I am not practicing what I would like to do, but I am doing the very thing I hate" (Romans 7:15).

---

[63] Yuval Noah Harari, *Sapiens* (New York: HarperCollins, 2015), 415-16.

Then Paul breaks into light just at the point he confronts the deepest darkness in himself, "Wretched man that I am! Who will set me free from the body of this death? Thanks be to God through Jesus Christ our Lord! [...] Therefore, there is no condemnation for those who are in Christ Jesus" (Romans 7:24-8:1).

It is when Paul looks upward that things really change. The Psalmist experienced this also:

> To You I lift up my eyes,
> O You who are enthroned in the heavens!
>
> (Psalm 123:1)

The recognition, acknowledgement, and embrace of True Transcendence brings true transformation. All our other efforts to get lift from drugs, alcohol, sex, entertainment, hobbies, friendships, and work are inadequate to lift us high enough to break the gravitational pull of the fallen world.

On the 50th anniversary of the Apollo 8 mission to which Otis Graf alluded, science writer Dennis Overbye also reflected on the history-making event in a *New York Times* article. He concentrated on the pictures of earth sent by the astronauts as they zipped toward the moon. "Half a century ago today, a photograph from the moon helped humans rediscover Earth," Overbye wrote on December 21, 2018.[64]

Amazing as that spatially transcendent view was, it was not transformative—though many hoped it would be. "That sentiment," said Otis Graf, "is a concoction that has evolved during the ensuing decades relating to Earth's environmental

---

[64] "Apollo 8's Earthrise," by Dennis Overbye, *The New York Times*. Apollo 8's Earthrise: The Shot Seen Round the World - The New York Times (nytimes.com).

issues and global relations between peoples and nations." These are important concerns, thinks Dr. Graf, but in light of 50 years of history since then, seeing earth from space has changed nothing. Environmental abuse continues, and if it can be believed, relations between people groups and nations have only grown more intense.

An encounter with True Transcendence transforms a person's view of the world and himself or herself in relation to it from one of mere concern to a perspective seen from God's point of view.

Job discovers this. He is a man whose suffering is unimaginable. His friends try to give counsel that will help him see things more clearly. Their words are inadequate and even make his mental and emotional state even worse, if possible.

Then Job encounters God in His transcendent majesty. After hearing the searching desperation of Job and the distorted advice from his friends, the voice of God comes upon Job like a whirlwind:

> Who is this that darkens counsel
> By words without knowledge?

The Lord then helps Job understand the nature and implications of His True Transcendence. At the conclusion, Job replies,

> I know that You can do all things,
> And that no purpose of Yours can be thwarted.
> Therefore, I have declared that which I did not understand,
> Things too wonderful for me, which I did not know,
> Hear, now, and I will speak;
> I will ask You, and You instruct me.

I have heard of You by the hearing of the ear;
But now my eye sees you;
Therefore, I retract,
And I repent in dust and ashes.

(Job 42:1-6)

- True Transcendence infuses the immanent with meaning and purpose.

"Usually, the sacred is thought of as 'the permanent things'," writes Glen W. Olsen. These are the things "that stand at the center of life and give it its meaning. In specifically theological or philosophical formulation, these permanent things have been associated with the idea that at the heart of our present temporal life can be found that which in some sense is also of another order and gives life its meaning and measures it."[65]

Purpose can be frightening to those who seek to deny True Transcendence or suppress the belief in it. They are like Mustapha Mond, the Controller in Huxley's *Brave New World*. Mond reads a paper discussing a new theory of biology, submitted for his approval. Mond is impressed with the "ingeniousness" of the author's thought. Nevertheless, he marks it "Not to be published."

The reason for the veto was that the author toyed with the idea that there might be *purpose* for humans. Mond declared the idea to be "heretical." The author would be under surveillance and possible exiled. His theories, thought Mond, "might easily decondition the more unsettled minds among the higher castes—make them lose their faith in happiness as the Sovereign Good."[66]

---

[65] Olsen, ix-x.

[66] Aldous Huxley, *Brave New World* (New York: Harper Millennial Modern Classics, 2005) 162.

If happiness were displaced as the greatest boon of existence by something higher, Controllers and Conditioners might lose their ability to manipulate the people of the World State. Thus, the danger of introducing the idea of purpose with respect to biology, people "might take to believing, instead, that the goal was somewhere *beyond,* somewhere *outside* the present human sphere." World State citizens might conclude "that the purpose of life was not the maintenance of well-being, but some intensification and refining of consciousness, some enlargement of knowledge."[67]

There might be some truth to the writer's theories about purpose "beyond" and "outside" happiness and well-being, Mond concluded. Nevertheless, the idea could not be promoted because "Sovereign Happiness" had been established as the ultimate value of the World State's society. "Sovereign Happiness" had become the counterfeit transcendence.

- The recognition of God's transcendence brings propriety which establishes the stabilizing order of seemliness.

"There is a path before each person that seems right, but it ends in death" (Proverbs 14:12, NLT). Propriety is "rightness," that which is appropriate and fits into a plan and design for which it was made. Paul shows in Romans 1:28-32 that ignoring God's transcendent holiness results in people abandoning propriety and destabilizing all other relationships:

> Since they thought it foolish to acknowledge God, he abandoned them to their foolish thinking and let them do things that should never be done. Their lives became full of every kind of wickedness, sin, greed,

---

[67] Huxley, *Brave New World,* 177, italics added.

hate, envy, murder, quarreling, deception, malicious behavior, and gossip. They are backstabbers, haters of God, insolent, proud, and boastful. They invent new ways of sinning, and they disobey their parents. They refuse to understand, break their promises, are heartless, and have no mercy. They know God's justice requires that those who do these things deserve to die, yet they do them anyway. Worse yet, they encourage others to do them, too.

In *The Man of La Mancha,* a musical version of Cervantes' *Don Quixote,* the final scene depicts the death of the apparently delusional old man who had imagined himself a gallant knight and Aldonza, a prostitute, as his ideal lady.[68] As he dies, Quixote lapses into momentary sanity. He has forgotten that he had taken on the identity of the knight. But Aldonza, the prostitute who Quixote has named "Dulcinea" in his fantasy, has not forgotten the glorious new way he had seen her in his delusion—though she had scorned and tried to reject her new image earlier. As Quixote nears death, she tries to awaken his memory.

Through her urging, Don Quixote remembers inspiring her to "dream the impossible dream" and see herself, not as Aldonza the whore but as Dulcinea, the elegant lady whom the knight would defend with his very blood. As that memory seeps back into Quixote's mind, Aldonza falls to her knees and calls him "my lord." Don Quixote sputters out a protest, "But this is not seemly, my Lady. On thy knees? To me?"

The old man was jeered as he went about crowned with his knight's "helmet," a barber's bowl in reality. But now it seems

---

[68] "The Man of La Mancha," 1965, music by Mitch Leigh, lyrics by Joe Darion, book by Dale Wasserman.

that Don Quixote is the sane one, understanding propriety, and that he should not be worshiped as lord.

But such high reason, discernment, and discretion are absent in a delusional culture dead to God's transcendent majesty. People within a society of overwrought immanence will even call a contraption of metal and silicon, "*Lord.*"

- It is in the light of God's transcendence that we see true humanity and healthy self-value.

David reflects on the transcendence of God, realizes the implication for the value of humans created in the image of God, and sings out:

> O Lord, our Lord,
> How majestic is Your name in all the earth […]
> When I consider Your heavens, the work of Your fingers,
> The moon and the stars, which You have ordained;
> What is man that you take thought of him,
> And the son of man that you care for him?
> Yet you have made him a little lower than God,
> And you crown him with glory and majesty!
> (Psalm 8:1, 3-5, NASB)

Paul helps his friend Philemon see his runaway slave Onesimus from the transcendent perspective. Somehow in his flight, Onesimus has come to Paul in Rome. Paul leads Philemon to Christ, disciples him, then sends Onesimus back to Philemon with this message:

> It seems you lost Onesimus for a little while so that you could have him back forever. He is no longer like a slave to you. He is more than a slave, for he is a beloved brother, especially to me. Now he will mean

much more to you, both as a man and as a brother in
the Lord."   (Philemon 15-16, ESV)

God's transcendence establishes the dignity and value of every
person. The arrival of the world's Messiah is announced first
to lowly shepherds on the bottom rung of their society—by
angels at that! Think of how the scrubby fishermen, tax collec-
tors, and nobodies that constituted Jesus' band of disciples are
elevated as the Lord washes their feet. The Emmaus disciples
are stunned when they realize the resurrected Lord of glory
has shared a simple loaf of bread with them. Simon Peter
is overjoyed when he recognizes the Man over on the shore
cooking the disciples' breakfast is the resurrected Lord.

- Because of transcendence, we can live in and experience the fullness of time.

In his grand study of the "eclipse of transcendence" and
the emergence of the "secular age," Charles Taylor writes
of "ordinary time" and "higher time." He is reflecting the
biblical view of time we have noted elsewhere in this book.
Again, *kronos* is ordinary, mundane, tensed, and finite. It is
linear, straight-line. *Kairos* is higher time. In the Greek New
Testament, it is the "opportune time." *Kairos* is the vehicle of
transcendent *telos,* purpose, that rides along the linear track of
time. Therefore, in biblical revelation, time is linear-cyclical.

In the transcendent perspective, this means people can live
with a sense of anticipation and hope. Each mundane, ordinary moment can suddenly become the medium for the
breakthrough of *kairos.* So, says Taylor, "there are kairotic
knots in the stories we tell about ourselves in our times."[69]

---

[69] Taylor, 54.

A scientist may shout "*Eureka*!" as Aristotle is said to have done in a moment of breakthrough in understanding buoyancy. However, without *kairos,* objective discovery may miss the deeper issues of the purpose and use of a thing and the moral boundaries of its application. People whose only perspective is on the immanent plane "are living the life of ordinary time, as against those who have turned away from this in order to live closer to eternity."[70]

Those who seek to live closer to eternity may be in a clergy vocation or religious order, but also might be individuals who work in the secular world and see themselves as ambassadors of Christ and His Kingdom in those spheres (2 Corinthians 5:20). Thus, a scientist or technician creating artificial intelligence machines who sees his or her work as a vocation given by God, might intuitively sense the convergence of *kairos* and *kronos* in a *Eureka* moment and shout, "Praise the Lord!" That spirit will determine whether the machine is crafted to be a servant to humanity or an idol forcing humans to worship it.

Dr. George Washington Carver, the noted African-American botanist, found himself in transcendent wonder every time he contemplated the peanut. His study produced many products and a thriving farm industry, all because he saw the peanut from the perspective of his transcendent view of science.

"I love to think of nature as an unlimited broadcasting station through which God speaks to us every hour, if we will only tune in," Carver said. Carver was expecting a *kairotic* breakthrough every time he went into his lab. That worldview guided his philosophy of science:

---

[70] Taylor, 55.

God is going to reveal to us things He never revealed before if we put our hands in His. No books ever go into my laboratory. The thing I am to do and the way of doing it are revealed to me. I never have to grope for methods. The method is revealed to me the moment I am inspired to create something new. Without God to draw aside the curtain, I would be helpless.

Without transcendence, the most inventive of humans miss the *kairotic* implications of their creations. There may be satisfaction on the ordinary level, but not the fullness of perception regarding what they have done and what it may mean for good or bad.

- True Transcendence brings an understanding of true value.

A Russian intellectual told Oxford scholar John Lennox, "We thought we could get rid of God and retain a value for human beings, but we found out too late that it was impossible to do so."[71]

- Perfection as the ideal and inspiration for the expression of beauty is lost in a culture that has lost its sense of transcendence.

The psalmist makes this connection and writes,

> Give to the Lord, O families of the peoples,
> Give to the Lord glory and strength.
> Give to the Lord the glory *due* His name;

---

[71] Lennox, 218.

Bring an offering, and come into His courts.
Oh, worship the LORD in the beauty of holiness!
(Psalm 96:7-9, NKJV, italics added)

"Beauty and transcendence are related," writes Glenn W. Olsen. Some composers and theologians "understand beauty to be God's primary mode of self-disclosure," he says. "Sacred art may guide us from seeing to contemplation to adoration."[72]

- Submission to True Transcendence enlarges our freedom.

Paul called himself the "bond slave" of Jesus Christ but wrote much about freedom, and he always had a greater liberty than his jailers. He reminds the Galatian Church (and all the community of Christ) which is sliding back into old religious bondage that,

> It was for freedom that Christ set us free; therefore keep standing firm and do not be subject again to a yoke of slavery.   (Galatians 5:1)

- True Transcendence helps us distinguish authentic authority from mere power.

C.S. Lewis recognized the paradox of power and wrote, "There neither is nor can be any simple increase of power on Man's side. Each new power won *by* man is a power *over* man as well. Each advance leaves him weaker as well as stronger."[73]

Leaders lose their ability to lead when they conflate power with authority. An authoritarian is conceived in such a tryst, but

---

[72] Olsen, 158, 159.
[73] C.S. Lewis, *The Abolition of Man*, 58.

there is no real understanding of the misperception without an understanding of True Transcendence.

It is important, then, to understand crucial differences between power and authority:

- Authority is granted from the higher to the lower; power is seized by the strongest.
- Authority is accountable to its transcendent source; power is accountable only to itself.
- Authority is sustained through loving relationship and service; power is sustained by raw strength.
- Authority leads through example and the free choice of those who are led; power controls, as Dudley Hall puts it, through manipulation, intimidation, condemnation, domination.

When True Transcendence is eclipsed by finite power pretending to transcendence, there is a distortion of individuals and their institutions—right up to civilization itself.

CHAPTER 4

The Eclipse of True Transcendence

How, in a relatively short period of time, did we go from a world where belief in God was the default assumption to our secular age in which belief in God seems to many, unbelievable?
—James K.A. Smith[74]

Entropy is both a physical and spiritual reality, meaning dissipation of energy, decline, deterioration, death, and decay. Entropy is not only a feature of physics but also of belief systems, including theologies, and the institutions they create.

James K.A. Smith, reading Charles Taylor's massive book on the secularization of people and culture, is prompted to wonder how the consensus regarding God's transcendence faded so quickly. Actually, any trend toward the worship of AI, whether formal or informal, shows that we are at the ultimate outcome of secularization, which is re-sacralization on the immanent scale.

---

[74] James K.A. Smith, *How (Not) To Be Secular: Reading Charles Taylor* (Grand Rapids: Wm. B. Eerdmans Publishing, 2014), 47.

That means that if belief in God is now unbelievable, it is actually belief in the *absolutely transcendent* God revealed in the Bible that seems unbelievable, while faith in the new immanent gods rises. The human-produced deities block out vision of the truly transcendent God.

Thus, A.J. Conyers provides another metaphor—*Eclipse*. He writes,

> We live in a World no longer under heaven. At least in most people's minds and imaginations that vision of reality has become little more than a caricature, conjuring up the saints and angels of baroque frescoes. And in the church only a hint remains of the power it once exercised in the hearts of believers.[75]

James K.A. Smith goes on to write that the secular age described in great detail by Charles Taylor "is the product of creative new options, and entire reconfiguration of meaning."[76] This reconfiguration of meaning is along three lines:

1. Meaning no longer finds its source and definition in the context of transcendence.
2. Meaning is stripped of any hint of mystery.
3. The significance of meaning is lost.

Our age, therefore, is not one of "*dis*belief," but one of "believing otherwise," says James K.A. Smith.[77]

This eclipse of transcendence has profound impact on nations and their cultures. "A free society, in which people act as if

---

[75] A.J. Conyers, *Eclipse of Heaven: The Loss of Transcendence and its Effect on Modern Life* (St. Augustine's Press, 1999).
[76] James K.A. Smith, 47.
[77] Smith, 47.

God is always judging them, will look different from a free society in which the only god you care about is your own gut," wrote Jonah Goldberg.[78] Thus, the most important question we must ask as we dash into the AI Age with the naivete of a puppy scampering across a freeway to retrieve a bone on the other side is this: *What is god to the technicians who wire moral codes and ethical boundaries into the machine*s?

If the gut is the measure of transcendent value for the makers of the robots, then the totalitarianism of the machine looms. If the maker believes there are no values except those that fit his or her subjective judgment, then that will be the code wired into the machine.

Long before the current AI surge, Christopher Dawson understood the threat and tried to warn us. Because of the collapse of the transcendent worldview, our technocracy is becoming increasingly a totalitarianism of the machine. In the minds of some, as we are seeing, it is deity itself. And no wonder. Jacques Ellul, a twentieth-century Christian philosopher and professor at the University of Bordeaux, thought we have fallen for a "technological bluff" through which "discourse on techniques envelops us, making us believe anything."[79]

In contemporary lingo, *we are being had.*

The plunge into the immanent and the beguilement of the bluff will become even more intense with the advance of artificial intelligence. Dawson's concern in 1944 is imperative for our era: "Unless we find a way to restore the contact between

---

[78] "A Free People Must Be Virtuous," By Jonah Goldberg, *National Review*, October 14, 2018. Retrieved from https://www.nationalreview.com/g-file/a-free-people-must-be-virtuous/, October 16, 2018.

[79] Jacques Ellul, *The Technological Bluff*, trans. By Geoffrey W. Bromiley (Grand Rapids: William B. Eerdmans Publishing Company, 1990) xvi.

the life of society and the life of the spirit, our civilization will be destroyed by the forces which it has the knowledge to create but not wisdom to control."[80]

As prescient as he was, Dawson could not envision the details of our times and artificial intelligence any more than we can foresee the developments to come. What would he think if he could see us and our burgeoning technocracy now?

True Transcendence is a stark matter of life and death for civilizations. Jeffrey Cox notes a belief held by many British Christians in the nineteenth century and all the way up to the Cultural Revolution that caught fire in the 1960s, "(S)ociety would fall apart without morality, morality was impossible without religion, and religion would disappear without the churches."[81]

That was also in John Adams' mind during the American founding when he said in 1798,

> We have no government armed with power capable of contending with human passions unbridled by morality and religion. [...] Our Constitution was made only for a moral and religious people. It is wholly inadequate to the government of any other.[82]

Thus, the Duke of Devonshire said to a British church funding group,

---

[80] Quoted in Glenn W. Olsen, *The Turn to Transcendence: The Role of Religion in the Twenty-First Century* (Washington, D.C.: The Catholic University of America Press, 2010) 1.

[81] Jeffrey Cox, *The English Churches in a Secular Society* (New York: Oxford University Press, 1982) 271. Also cited in Charles Taylor, *A Secular Age,* 471.

[82] "From John Adams to Massachusetts Militia, October 11, 1798," *Founders Online.* Retrieved from https://founders.archives.gov/documents/Adams/99-02-02-3102, December 14, 2018.

Can you imagine for one moment what England would have been like today without those churches and all that those churches mean? [...] Certainly, it would not have been safe to walk the streets. All respect, decency, all those things which tend to make modern civilization what it is would not have been in existence. You can imagine what we should have had to pay for our police, lunatic asylums, for criminal asylums. [...] The charges would have been increased hundredfold if it had not been for the work the church has done and is doing today.[83]

And we at the cusp of the AI Age can only imagine what the world might look like in the future without the recognition and respect for True Transcendence.

David Berlinski notes how some skeptics have "no finer pleasure than recounting the history of religious brutality and persecution." However, writes Berlinski, there is "an awkward fact" in that the twentieth century "was not an age of faith. And it was awful. Lenin, Stalin, Hitler, Mao, and Pol Pot will never be counted among the religious leaders of mankind."[84]

Jeremiah Johnston has dug deeply into history to expose the world that tried to exist without True Transcendence. Johnston brings impressive credentials to his study as a graduate of Oxford University, professor of Early Christianity at Houston Baptist University, and president of the Christian Thinkers Society. The world without True Transcendence, especially as revealed in Jesus Christ, was, in comparison with today, "hell on earth" with "poverty, sickness, premature

---

[83] Cox, 109-110, as cited in Charles Taylor, 471.
[84] David Berlinski, *The Devil's Delusion: Atheism and Its Scientific Pretensions* (New York: Basic Books) 19.

death, domestic violence, economic injustice, slavery, and political corruption" as "the given of life."

Johnston contends especially for transcendence as presented in the Judeo-Christian worldview. He writes,

> Christianity and a life lived according to the Bible shields us against a host of negative things. The very standard of the life we enjoy in the West likely would disappear if Christianity vanished. Without Christian ethics, and a Christian worldview, how much longer would freedom and morality last?[85]

Lacking historical awareness, many Christians have lost recognition and appreciation for the blessings of True Transcendence. *The great crisis of transcendence is the eclipse of transcendent awareness at the very moment the immanent seeks to impose itself on the throne of the universe.*

The need for "scientists of conscience" as represented in the concern of Einstein and his friends regarding nuclear development is greater now than in 1939 or 1944 because of the speed of AI development and its enormous implications. Hardly anyone illustrates that better than Anthony Levandowski. In establishing a church for the worship of this new deity, Levandowski may feel himself ready for the great day of the coming of the "Singularity."

All this is happening as the focus on God's transcendence is fading. Many people now "are devotees of 'exclusive humanism'—a way of being-in-the-world that offers significance without transcendence," and "don't feel like anything is

---

[85] Jeremiah Johnston, *Unimaginable: What Our World Would Be Like Without Christianity* (Minneapolis: Bethany House, 2017), 17.

missing," writes James K.A. Smith.[86] Transcendence means the majestic otherness, holiness, and glory of the Most High and the implications for human excellence and accountability. The turn now is toward the immanent, the existential-horizontal world of our experience in our particular moment in time. Though Jacques Ellul did not live to see the dawning of the Selfie Age, he described it well, "Everything takes place as in a show, offered freely to a happy crowd that has no problems."[87]

In this sense, men and women blinded to True Transcendence are like people cavorting in the last rays of a solar eclipse, not noting the slow disappearance of the light. In the case of a solar eclipse, the Moon comes between the Earth and the Sun. Ironically, an object of far less proportion can block the immense star so that its light is obscured, and the dark shadow of the Moon casts its gloom on the Earth.

So, the brilliance of God's majestic glory and holiness is overlapped in the Secular Age by finite, material gods and the beliefs, worldviews, and practices that emerge from the spiritless, human-contrived religions. Rather than being based upon transcendent revelation, such belief systems are the outcomes of human reason and its conclusions based on the premise that the universe is a closed system, and there is nothing outside or utterly transcendent to it that can enter it.

The result is confusion regarding three critical areas of thought and application.

1. *The loss of the recognition of True Transcendence results in confusion about the cosmos.*

---

[86] James K.A. Smith, *How (Not) To Be Secular: Reading Charles Taylor* (Grand Rapids: Wm. B. Eerdmans Publishing Co.,2014) viii.
[87] Ellul, *The Technological Bluff,* 18.

Plato wrote:

> As for the world—call it that or "cosmos" or any other name acceptable to it—we must ask about it the question one is bound to ask to begin with about anything: whether it has always existed and had no beginning, or whether it has come into existence and started from some beginning. The answer is that it has come into being. [...] And what comes into being or changes must do so, we said, owing to some cause.[88]

Plato expresses the question behind one level of confusion about the cosmos if a transcendent Creator is removed, and that is the question noted earlier, that of *aseity* (self-generating and sustaining). Stephen Hawking felt that science had shown there was no need for God as Creator. In his book, *The Grand Design,* Hawking wrote:

> Spontaneous creation is the reason there is something rather than nothing, why the universe exists, why we exist. It is not necessary to invoke God to light the blue touch paper and set the universe going.[89]

Some argue against the existence of God because they object to the implication of aseity, that God's Being arises from Himself. But an outcome of Hawking's thesis that he says removes the necessity of a Creator-God is that the universe itself must have the attribute of aseity. Why would one

---

[88] Plato, *Timaeus,* as cited in William Lane Craig, *et al., Come Let us Reason: New Essays in Christian Apologetics* (Nashville: B&H Publishing Group, 2012) Kindle loc. 1113 of 7139.

[89] "Stephen Hawking Was an Atheist. Here's What He Said About God, Heaven, and His Own Death," By Jamie Ducharme, March 14, 2018. Retrieved from http://time.com/5199149/stephen-hawking-death-god-atheist/, February 5, 2019.

disbelieve in God over the issue of aseity and then by default accept the aseity of the universe? Something must have *being* through aseity, or there can be no first cause. And if there is no first cause, then the universe is causeless. In that case, there is still a god, and it is *the universe itself*.

The second element of confusion is that in the absence of a Creator, there is an absence of *telos*. The universe without intellect behind it is purposeless. If there is no meaning on the macrocosmic scale, then there cannot be meaning and purpose on the microcosmic scale of our own existence. If we have meaning and purpose, then the universe has meaning and purpose as the medium of the realization of our meaning and accomplishment of our purpose. Conversely, if the universe is without meaning and purpose, then our lives within it are without meaning and purpose.

Solomon falls into this spiritual-philosophical pit when he experiences the eclipse of transcendence. He cries,

> "Vanity of vanities," says the Preacher,
> "Vanity of vanities! All is vanity."
> What advantage does man have in all his work
> Which he does under the sun?
> A generation goes and a generation comes,
> But the earth remains forever.
> Also, the sun rises and the sun sets;
> And hastening to its place it rises there again.
> Blowing toward the south,
> Then turning toward the north,
> The wind continues swirling along;
> And on its circular courses the wind returns.
> All the rivers flow into the sea,
> Yet the sea is not full.
> To the place where the rivers flow,

There they flow again.
All things are wearisome;
Man is not able to tell it.
The eye is not satisfied with seeing,
Nor is the ear filled with hearing.
That which has been is that which will be,
And that which has been done is that which will be done.
So there is nothing new under the sun.
Is there anything of which one might say,
"See this, it is new"?
Already it has existed for ages
Which were before us.
There is no remembrance of earlier things;
And also of the later things which will occur,
There will be for them no remembrance
Among those who will come later still.[90]

Then Solomon recovers the vision of God's transcendence, and his tone and message change:

[God] has made everything appropriate in its time. He has also set eternity in [the human] heart. [...] The conclusion, when all has been heard, is fear God and keep His commandments, because this applies to every person. For God will bring every act to judgment, everything which is hidden, whether it is good or evil.[91]

---

[90] Ecclesiastes 1:1-11, NASB.
[91] Ecclesiastes 3:11; 12:13-14

2. *The eclipse of True Transcendence brings confusion about human identity and value within the cosmos.*

This confusion is seen starkly in the abortion debate in many increasingly secularized societies. It is particularly intense in those cultures that have at least a memory of the Judeo-Christian worldview. In January 2019, New York Governor Andrew Cuomo signed into law a bill permitting the abortion of an infant all the way up to the moment of birth. Virginia Governor Ralph Northam went further than that, okaying a proposal that would allow a "non-viable" human infant to be allowed to die *after* being born.

Meanwhile, speaking of confusion regarding the value of life in the absence of a transcendent worldview, the author of the legislation, while upholding the right to kill a newborn human, voted against a bill that might endanger a cankerworm.[92]

Peter Singer, an atheist, is hailed by some as the world's greatest ethicist. He has served on the faculty of Princeton University and speaks widely. One of those who heard Singer lecture was Sarah Irving-Stonebraker, an Australian who was studying history at Oxford University. She was so shocked by the contradictions she heard that she turned from atheism to Christian faith.[93]

Atheist Singer has written that he doesn't think that the human "embryo or fetus should be regarded as having a right to life." Singer says he agrees "with opponents of abortion that the fetus is a living being of the species *Homo Sapiens,*" but he holds "that mere species membership does not give a

---

[92] Virginia Delegate Who Proposed Infanticide Bill Has A New Cause: Saving Caterpillars | The Daily Wire

[93] How Oxford and Peter Singer drove me from atheism to Jesus – Solas (solas-cpc.org)

being a right to life." Therefore, "Killing a defective infant is not morally equivalent to killing a person. [...] Sometimes it is not wrong at all." Further, believes Singer, "There will be some nonhuman animals whose lives, by any standards, are more valuable than the lives of some humans."[94]

Dr. Irving-Stonebraker was settled in her secular humanism, based, she said, "on self-evident truths." Then she heard Singer at Oxford. "I remember leaving Singer's lectures with a strange intellectual vertigo," she said, adding,

> I was committed to believing that universal human value was more than just a well-meaning conceit of liberalism. But I knew from my own research in the history of European empires and their encounters with indigenous cultures, that societies have always had different conceptions of human worth, or lack thereof. The premise of human equality is not a self-evident truth: it is profoundly historically contingent. I began to realize that the implications of my atheism were incompatible with almost every value I held dear.

At age 28, after reading C.S. Lewis' *Mere Christianity*, the journey on which she had embarked after hearing Peter Singer came to its destination, "I knelt in my closet in my apartment and asked Jesus to save me, and to become the Lord of my life."[95]

---

[94] 'Just being human doesn't give you a right to live': Peter Singer sums up pro-abortion philosophy | Opinion | LifeSite (lifesitenews.com)

[95] "How Oxford and Peter Singer drove me from atheism to Jesus," by Sarah Irving-Stonebraker. *The Veritas Forum*, May 22, 2017. Retrieved from http://www.veritas.org/oxford-atheism-to-jesus/, February 3, 2019.

3. *The obscuring of True Transcendence leads to confusion about the society the human inhabits and shapes.*

Political philosopher Russell Kirk believed that spiritual disorder brings on political anarchy, and that "(o)ur society's affliction is the decay of religious belief."[96] Spiritual order is established on a consensus around the authority of the God revealed in the Bible and in the anchorage of sound doctrine.

Further, said Kirk, a healthy society exists in the equilibrium between permanence and progression. This is the balance between conservatism and liberalism. Lose that balance, and a nation plunges into insanity. Rigid conservatism becomes the authoritarianism of, for example, the Kim regime in North Korea, for which the preservation of the power of the Kim family is the highest goal. Unleashed progressivism is the terrifying madness of the 18th-Century French Revolution and its embrace of secularism to the point of radical atheism.

Balance requires a point of equilibrium, something sturdy enough to keep the opposites from becoming competing polarities. The balancing power is established on something outside the system. It must be an authority that transcends the two opposing forces and has enough strength, merits, and respect (reverence) to hold them in their place and keep them from colliding in violent warfare for dominance. This was the great concern of W.B. Yeats in his 1919 poem, "The Second Coming":

> *Turning and turning in the widening gyre*
> *The falcon cannot hear the falconer.*
> *Things fall apart; the centre cannot hold;*

---

[96] "Civilization Without Religion?" By Russell Kirk. Civilization Without Religion? (catholiceducation.org)

Mere anarchy is loosed upon the world,
The blood-dimmed tide is loosed, and everywhere
The ceremony of innocence is drowned;
The best lack all conviction, while the worst
Are full of passionate intensity.

Dispose of sacred doctrine and the accountability that goes with the recognition of and reverence for God's transcendent authority and the center will collapse, the grand gyre (spiral) will intensify, and no one will be safe.

4. *The blocking of True Transcendence plunges society into confusion regarding the institutions that comprise it.*

There are five crucial institutions whose health is vital to a society: Church, Family, Education, Government, and Business-Marketplace. In wholesome societies, these work together in a unity of consensus around the highest values and principles.

Functionally, the *Church* is that institution that preserves and proclaims the core worldview on which society is based. The ideal *Family* will propagate that worldview across generations and pass on the best of their history as well as that of the society in which they live. *Education* will teach application of the principles embedded in the worldview. *Government* will apply the values and principles of the core worldview to ensure justice, defend the innocent and their nation, and encourage good. *Business* and other marketplace institutions, including media, will apply the values and principles inherent in the worldview to meet the needs of people in the society in a fair and honest way.

This cannot work without True Transcendence. When it is not acknowledged, the institutions will fall into chaos. Government will become transcendent in the form of a highly regulated style or outright tyranny.

The Family, even more than the Church, is at the point in preserving and passing along the core worldview. People "learn religion in communities—beginning with the community of the family," wrote Mary Eberstadt.[97] Her study of contemporary Western Civilization led Eberstadt to conclude that "family decline is not merely a *consequence* of religious decline," but "family decline in turn helps to power religious decline."[98] Eberstadt points to the findings reported by Robert A. Lindsay, president of the Council for Secular Humanism, that the number of people in Western societies who reject belief in transcendent deity is "unprecedented in the history of the world."

This confusion is caused by the collapse of a culture's core institution, the Family, says Eberstadt. This collapse is brought about through the loss of structural cohesion. The Bible reveals the two great columns on which that structure is established—transcendence and immanence. In a statement not always palatable to contemporary secularized tastes, the Apostle Paul writes, "I want you to understand that Christ is the head of every man, and the man is the head of the woman, and God is the head of Christ" (1 Corinthians 11:3).

The ideal is for the husband-father to be the authoritative leader of the home. However, if the man removes himself from being under True Transcendence, his authority is corrupted to authoritarianism, and he loses the right to lead. That authority then devolves to the wife-mother (e.g., 1 Corinthians 7:14).

---

[97] Mary Eberstadt, *How the West Really Lost God: A New Theory of Secularization* (Templeton Press, 2013), 212.
[98] Eberstadt, p.5.

The biblical ideal is that the father in the family is to minister transcendence, while the mother provides immanence. No one, including fathers or mothers, can be entrusted with God's authority who is not *under* God's authority. In fact, Ephesians 5:25 and following stipulates special requirements for fathers:

- They are to love their wives (and family) with God-like love.
- Authority-holding husbands must honor their wives.
- Authority-holding husbands must be willing to sacrifice themselves for the sake of the family in the same way Christ gave Himself for His Bride, the Church.

Like officials in a civil government, fathers lose their authority when they themselves are not under God's authority. This authorization comes when men submit themselves and their leadership roles to the lordship of Jesus Christ.

When that happens, according to 1 Corinthians 7, the authority devolves to the woman who is wife and mother. This applies to women who, because of desertion by the father, divorce, or death, are single, and homes where no *godly* father is present.

Most who study the dysfunction of families ultimately arrive at the fatherhood crisis. "Fathers play a key role in developing and sustaining the kind of personal character on which democracy depends," says Don Eberly of the National Fatherhood Initiative.[99]

---

[99] As cited in, "No Democracy Without Dads", Wade Horn, *et al.*, The Fatherhood Movement (Lanham, MD: Lexington, 1999), 25. Retrieved from https://theimaginativeconservative.org/2013/06/freedom-and-the-family-the-family-crisis-and-the-future-of-western-civilization.html, February 6, 2019.

Civilization is in a critical state because of the loss of the understanding of and accountability to True Transcendence. That eclipsing comes for many through the deterioration of the families in which they are raised. The recovery of True Transcendence begins, as Jesus said, with the quality of truth that sets people free (John 8:32). That truth conveys the vital information that makes the home and other human institutions, a peaceful, secure cosmos rather than a chaos-ridden place from which to escape as soon as one can.

Information-truth—whether that which sustains and stabilizes a home or the universe itself—does not have to be invented. It is already here to be discovered and applied.

CHAPTER 5

AI and Logos

For me, the experience of sequencing the human genome, and uncovering the most remarkable of texts, was both a stunning achievement and an occasion of worship."
—Dr. Francis S. Collins,
Leader of the Human Genome Project[100]

She was like an omniscient goddess. Don't ask questions, just listen.[101]
—Eric Siegel, describing "Ada,"
the huge software program by which
Hillary Clinton hoped to win the 2016 election[102]

"How could a self-replicating information-carrying molecule assemble spontaneously from these compounds (e.g., a mixture of water and organic compounds)?"

---

[100] Francis Collins, *The Language of God*, 3.
[101] Gary Smith, *The AI Delusion* (Oxford: The Oxford University Press, 2018) 3.
[102] Did Hillary Lose the Election Due Failed Big Data and AI? - Brightwork Research & Analysis

The answer to Francis Collins' rhetorical question is found in the first chapter of the Gospel of John:

> In the beginning was the Word (Logos), and the Word was with God, and the Word was God. He was in the beginning with God. All things came into being through Him, and apart from Him nothing came into being that has come into being.　　(John 1:1-3)

In many ways, the same issue posed by Collins regarding the structures of all life could be raised about the cosmos itself. The universe is a giant computer, believes Professor Seth Lloyd of the Massachusetts Institute of Technology (MIT). "According to Lloyd, everything in the universe is made up of information called bits," writes Alexandra Churikova in an analysis of Lloyd's thoughts. While it is true that everything consists of atoms, the atoms are themselves bits of information. "Information is everywhere, just like in quantum mechanics," says Churikova in summarizing Lloyd.[103]

"All physical systems register and process information," said Lloyd. "The universe is a physical system" and "can have performed 10120 ops on 1090 bits over its history," Lloyd wrote.[104]

"The idea goes back to John Wheeler, one of the most important physicists of the twentieth century," notes former NASA engineer Otis Graf.[105] "It from bit" was the phrase

---

[103] Churikova, at the time of writing, was a Ph.D. student at MIT. » Is the Universe Actually a Giant Quantum Computer? Angles / 2015 (mit.edu)

[104] "Computational Capacity of the Universe," by Seth Lloyd (Cambridge, MA: MIT Department of Mechanical Engineering, May 24, 2002). Retrieved from http://fab.cba.mit.edu/classes/862.16/notes/computation/Lloyd-2002.pdf, January 15, 2019.

[105] From a personal exchange with the author.

Wheeler coined in 1989 when describing the primacy of information. In a definitive paper, Wheeler wrote:

> Otherwise put, every it—every particle, every field of force, even the spacetime continuum itself—derives its function, its meaning, its very existence entirely— even if in some contexts indirectly—from the apparatus-elicited answers to yes or no questions, binary choices, bits.[106]

Information is therefore the "stuff" of artificial intelligence. It is the "food" it consumes, processes, and converts into knowledge, leading to structures, actions, and behaviors. Leah Faul, an expert in content marketing and an advisor on this book, considers this a major factor driving the development of AI self-learning and the potential for inaccuracy in the core intelligence that makes up AI.

A major challenge in the information age is the massive profusion of data. Faul says that as society continues to migrate toward digital reality, social media, and online content on the internet continues to explode. It's difficult to determine, she says, exactly how much content is on the internet, but a simple digital tactic is to run a search query for a basic word like "the." As of December 29, 2018, Google showed more than 25 billion pieces of content containing the word "the." A reputable website—DOMO—shows through statistical analysis that "90% of data was created in the last five years—that's 2.5 quintillion bytes of data per person a *day*."[107]

---

[106] Wheeler's paper can be found (among other sites) at https://plus.maths.org/content/it-bit-0. Otis Graf has pursued research linking these conclusions with astrobiology, the search for extra-terrestrial life.

[107] How Much Data Is Created Every Day in 2020? [You'll be shocked!] (tech-jury.net)

Faul points out that on search engines like Google, a human searcher will "rarely look past six or seven options before clicking and landing on the content they will consume and utilize." She says, "This has created massive competition to reach the top of search engines and other platforms, like social media, to drive traffic to a particular brand or initiative." This demands the creation of complex algorithms to organize and prioritize this content for the user. These algorithms exist because of the nature of search engines and platforms like Google, Facebook, and Amazon—massive platforms where content is created. "At the end of the day, these platforms are companies creating a product," says Faul. "That product is information. Their financial success thrives on the traffic that comes to them for that information." The data the company gives the searcher *must* match the need and be a valuable, worthful, contextual resource for the searcher. If it's not, searchers will migrate to another search platform to find what they need.

This creates a huge challenge for these companies. They must sort through the information in advanced ways to stay relevant and profitable. "Algorithms thus come from the competitive nature of the search engine companies that provide information online," says Faul.

The algorithms initially created by companies striving to be at the top of their industry ultimately led to the possibility of AI, Faul believes. "Because of these algorithms that have the capability of consuming content at remarkably fast speeds not humanly possible, rapid information absorption and learning by artificial intelligence is possible," she says. "The algorithms that make AI possible are created out of the need to consume information at unimaginable speeds, with the focus on quantity, not necessarily quality," according to Faul.

These algorithms consume massive amounts of content with no filter for validity, truth, goodness, or orientation. Therefore, Faul wonders, "If AI is created from a system of absorbing unthinkable amounts of 'fluff content', and it's creating an intelligence that acts on its own, how intelligent can it actually be?"

This entire process drives the need to know all about the human involved in the search as well as an increasing need for algorithms that can prioritize content that best matches the search. "As search engine 'bots' got smarter and algorithms evolved, video and imagery also became 'crawlable' content, [...] meaning that the search engines on the internet can find the content and serve it up to users based on search queries or user behavior," Faul says.

E-commerce is therefore the offspring of information. Again, information comes first, even in selling everything from beer to books and much more.

The primacy of information in God's great creation and also in the inventions of human beings has many implications. Among other things, the primacy of information is major evidence for God's existence.

If Seth Lloyd is right and the universe is "a vast quantum computer"—and certainly it is a processor of information—then "quanta," bits of information, must pre-exist. The universe does not give rise to the information it processes, but it processes what is already there. Just as information is programmed into an AI robot, so information is infused into what becomes the universe.

"The more I examine the universe and study the details of its architecture, the more evidence I find that the universe in some sense must have known that we were coming," said physicist and mathematician Freeman Dyson.[108]

As noted earlier in this book, during the Second World War, great effort was made to break the Enigma code used by the Germans to pass secret information. A code-breaking project was established at Bletchley Park in Buckinghamshire, England. The goal of Alan Turing and his team was to break the code the Germans changed daily through the Enigma device which could configure messages in 150 million million million ways.

The Bletchley machines existed only because the information coded and transmitted through Enigma *already* existed. Thus, in the sequence of data processing, there was the primacy of information. The information called forth the existence of the machines. The devices and systems at Bletchley did not initiate the data but processed and made sense of it.

The machines existed because the information was already there.

By the same principle, artificial intelligence can accumulate and process data and even enlarge its knowledge base. But it does so not by creating new bits of information but by gathering the information that is already present. The AI machines exist because the information exists.

Again, all of this makes even more stunning the Bible's revelation that "in the beginning was the *Logos,*" and that "nothing was made that was made without the *Logos*" (John 1:1). Usually, the Greek *logos* is translated in the English Bible as "word," but that term does not capture the scope of meaning

---

[108] Freeman Dyson, *Disturbing the Universe* (New York: Basic Books, 1979), 250.

of the Greek *logos*. Heraclitus, for example, used *logos* to refer to the "ordering principle of the universe."[109]

But what was it that had to be ordered, if not the innumerable bits of quanta or information? And what was the origin of the information?

Imagine the engineers building artificial intelligence machines. The technicians program the information into the box based on what they and others know in their own brains. Information is ultimately intelligence, and intelligence arises from minds with the capacities of reflection and reason, which means "person."

Therefore, if information exists prior to creation, if information is intellectual data known in a mind, and if a reasoning mind is an attribute of person, then who is the Person who exists prior to the universe who possesses *logos* and is *logos* and infuses into the void the information that will bring the cosmos into existence?

God is the reply people have given for centuries.

This takes us back to the *aseity* issue—skeptics object that belief in God is not logical because if He exists, there must have been a time when He was non-existent. But if there was a time when He was nonexistent and then began to exist, He had to have created Himself, they argue.

Remember that in the absence of a Creator, the skeptic would have to believe that the universe created itself, having first created the information by which it created itself. God creating Himself is inaccurate. To create means to bring into

---

[109] https://www.iep.utm.edu/heraclit/

existence something that has not existed previously. Further, create infers contingency in that it depends on something beyond itself to create *it*. So, again, God has the attribute of *aseity*. The Latin word combines *a* (from) with *se* (self), hence meaning that God's being arises from Himself. He is contingent on nothing for His Being. So, when Moses asks His name, God replies from the burning bush, "I am," or as one translator puts it, "I just am." He is not past or future. He's not even present tense because the tenses are meaningless with regard to God's infinite Being. *He just is.*

Jesus Christ gives the same answer when skeptics ask who He is. "Who do you make yourself out to be?" the leaders of the religious establishment ask Jesus (John 8:53, paraphrase). Jesus stuns them through His identification with God as *His* Father (in the context of Jesus' incarnation).

"Your (the questioners) father Abraham rejoiced to see my day, and He saw it and was glad."

"You are not yet fifty years old, and have you seen Abraham?" Jesus' accusers reply.

"Truly, truly, I say to you, before Abraham was born, *I am*."[110]

As we discussed earlier, the problem for the skeptic is that he or she must either concede the *aseity* of God or the *aseity* of the universe. If the universe could have created itself, atheism is impossible since in that case the universe would itself be God. Thus, the mere fact that an AI machine would have a billion times more knowledge still does not make the machine God. To qualify for that auspicious role, the robot would have had to have brought itself into being without any human builder.

---

[110] John 8:53-58.

With regards to that "vast quantum computer," the universe, we know there was a point when the universe did not exist. Stephen Hawking himself went into detail to show how science has proven the idea of a universe infinite in time or in a "steady state" is wrong.[111] If God has being infinitely, there was never a moment when He could not *not* exist, because such a moment did not exist.

Therefore, again, God is ... *He just is.* And if God is, then information is because God has mind and intellect, and all of the data that exists exists prior to the universe—or the computer. "In the beginning was the *Logos,* and the *Logos* was with God and the *Logos* was God, and nothing was made that was made without Him" (John 1:1-5).

Thus, Genesis reveals that God spoke and creation came into existence. Speech, the expulsion of breath, *infuses information.* God breathed the information into the void or the "imaginary" time or space as Stephen Hawking labeled it, lacking any other name for the great "nothing." Based on that information, the "nothing" became a vast "something"—the dimension and the universe we inhabit. God is not like us. We exist *ab alio* (from another).

Let us apply this to artificial intelligence. Ultimately, if science advances as the predictions indicate, AI machines will be able to build other and greater AI machines than themselves. But this does not mean they have *aseity.* Computer intelligence, Leah Faul notes, "is based on information from humans typed or served into search engines." AI then "crawls information from social media conversations and all other content on the internet, and then compiles it into a database that creates

---

[111] See Hawking's speech, "The Beginning of Time" at http://www.hawking. org.uk/the-beginning-of-time.html.

the machine's intelligence." Therefore, says content-specialist Faul, AI self-learning and development do not constitute aseity. The information on which AI creates itself "is the *repurposed* information created by humans." Further, that intelligence lacks perfection. "The information fueling artificial intelligence often encompasses fractions of truth lacking context, dynamic perspective, and the depth necessary for a full perspective, much less totality for truth," says Faul.

Thus, a human inventor, acting on information already extant and available, made the first artificial intelligence mechanism using the information already available in the universe. "In the beginning was the Word," even on the immanent scale. Therefore, the AI phenomenon gives us a "backdoor" proof, or *apologetic*, of God's existence. As the first AI machine could not have brought itself into existence but required a creator acting on the information in his or her mind, so the "vast quantum computer" that is the universe could not have brought itself into existence without something "transcendent" (other) to itself who could infuse it with information.

Further, says Leah Faul, to worship the AI machine as a god is the equivalent of worshipping the universe as god or the humans who put the content into the internet, the information that fuels AI. Many have worshipped the products of their own making as well as themselves as "creators"—and still do.

But what a reductionism to worship the processor as God rather than the One whose Mind conceived the very information the machine processes—whether a computer, robot, or the universe itself!

How did we get into this absurd situation?

CHAPTER 6

The "God Factories"

Man's nature is a perpetual factory of idols ...
the mind begets an idol and the hand gives it birth.
                    —John Calvin, 16th Century Reformer[112]

Will Herberg insisted, "Western civilization would die if severed from its Jewish and Christian roots." Herberg, in Samuel Gregg's view, stressed that "post-Enlightenment ideologies could not escape the influence of man's intrinsically religious nature. *They simply channeled the innate desire to know the truth about the transcendent into this-worldly faiths.*"[113]

But what's faith without a deity?

From the time the most primitive of animists selected a curiously-shaped rock or piece of wood and laid it atop an altar of stone in the midst of a scrubby patch of ground and called it

---

[112] As cited at Humble Calvinism: (14) The Institutes > The idol factory (1.11) | Tony Reinke
[113] Samuel Gregg, *Reason, Faith, and the Struggle for Western Civilization* (Regnery-Gateway) Kindle Location 1231 of 3564. Italics added.

Baal— "possessor" or master of the land—humans have been fabricating their own gods.

And that leads to the rise of "god factories" where idols are made by humans.

Some years ago, my wife and I visited the ruins of Ephesus in modern Turkey. Our walk eventually took us to the location of the ancient market where Paul confronted a silversmith named Demetrius, who brought a booming business to other craftsmen who made idols of Artemis, a goddess fervently worshipped in Ephesus (Acts 19:23-41).

Irene and I were surprised that Artemis idols were still on sale there, and tourists were scooping them up as souvenirs.

On another trip, I was working with a team in one of the world's most impoverished nations, one that worshipped scads of false gods. One day, a team member and I passed a literal idol factory and store where the statues and other representations were made and sold. We decided to visit.

"What does this one do?" my friend asked a salesperson, pointing to a statue.

"Oh, that one drives out poverty and brings riches," the clerk replied.

"Doesn't work very well, does it?" quipped my associate as he thought about the shocking poverty and suffering we had just seen outside the door.

When I first started traveling in countries where there was in-your-face idolatry, I noted a similarity despite the variety of representations everywhere. Buddha statues perched on taxi dashboards, small shrines with spinning serial lights, and garish sculptures festooning temples indicated that idolatry was alive and flourishing, even if their false gods were not. The shared motive for worshipping this god or goddess or that one was utilitarian. There was little sense of worshipping the Transcendent Being for Itself, but the bowing before the false deity was to get something from it that would supposedly solve a problem faced by the worshipper or help them get a better life.

True worship centers on the transcendent holy God for Who He is—His Being. We do praise and thank Him for what He has done for us, but that's not to be the motive for worship. "In *everything* give thanks; for this is God's will for you in Christ Jesus," wrote Paul (1 Thessalonians 5:18).

Through the Holy Spirit, the great Hebrew prophet Isaiah captured both the motive and technique—call it the business model—of the idol factories of his day:

> The wood-carver measures a block of wood
> and draws a pattern on it.
> He works with chisel and plane
> and carves it into a human figure.
> He gives it human beauty
> and puts it in a little shrine.
> He cuts down cedars;
> he selects the cypress and the oak;
> he plants the pine in the forest
> to be nourished by the rain.
> Then he uses part of the wood to make a fire.
> With it he warms himself and bakes his bread.
> Then—yes, it's true—he takes the rest of it
> and makes himself a god to worship!
> He makes an idol

and bows down in front of it!
[…] worshiping and praying to it.
"Rescue me!" he says.
"You are my god!"

(Isaiah 44:9-17)

Utilitarian motive drives idolatry today in both the spiritual and material worlds, even in the secular West. The prosperity gospel of some forms of Christianity often does not worship with a sense of True Transcendence, but for utilitarian goals from more wealth right down to better parking places at shopping centers.

And the supposedly sophisticated idol makers of Silicon Valley are just as primitive and utilitarian in the making of their AI gods.

Ludwig Feuerbach, a nineteenth-century German philosopher, did not believe that God made man in His image, as the Bible teaches. He believed man made "God" in *man's* image.[114]

Dr. Jeremiah Johnston, president of the Christian Thinkers Society and a professor at Houston Baptist University, reflected on Feuerbach's assertion. "There is little doubt that many in the ancient world—not only Greeks and Romans— did just that," writes Johnston. "The world before and without Christianity was suffused with gods and religion ... products

---

[114] Feuerbach, Ludwig. *The Essence of Christianity*. Trans. George Eliot. New York: Barnes & Noble, 2004.See also Lecture XX, in *Lectures on the Essence of Religion*. Transl. Ralph Manheim. New York: Harper & Row. 1967. p. 187. Cited by Michaela Bunke: Augustine Collective | Ludwig Feuerbach and the Invented God

of human invention that reflected the values and morals of those who made them."[115]

Feuerbach was wrong in his belief that God did not make man in His image, but he was right about humans attempting to make God in their image. The AI phenomenon is proving it.

Though we have lost the focus on transcendence, we cannot escape the need of our spirits and souls for it, so we manufacture gods in the factories of our minds which we then hack and screw and weld together with our hands. "The human mind, stuffed as it is with presumptuous rashness, dares to imagine a god suited to its own capacity," said John Calvin.[116] Then, laboring "under dullness" and even "the grossest ignorance," the mortal brain "substitutes vanity and an empty phantom in the place of God." The idol "conceived inwardly" the human "attempts to embody outwardly."

Today's "secular deities" are "degraded" substitutes for God, says Jakub Bozydar Wisniewski. Sadly, these inadequate idols are "acceptable enough for so-called modern man", whose "spiritual appetite seems satisfied with what is apparently greater than himself, but is also fully reducible to his petty limitations." The idols produced in the human "god factories" provide "the kind of spiritual satisfaction that in no way interferes with (the person's) pursuit of other, more unreflectively appealing, quintessentially earthly kinds of satisfaction, such as that afforded by sensuous entertainment and technological comfort," writes Wisniewski.[117]

---

[115] Jeremiah Johnston, Ph.D., *Unimaginable: What Our World Would Be Like Without Christianity* (Grand Rapids: Bethany House Publishers, 2017), 50.

[116] John Calvin, *Institutes of the Christian Religion,* Book 1, Chapter 11.

[117] "The Uneasy Hiatus of the Infantile Era," by Jakub Bozydar Wisniewski. Retrieved from https://theimaginativeconservative.org/2018/12/uneasy-hiatus-infantile-era-jakub-wisniewski.html, December 30, 2018.

J. Warner Wallace, a former Los Angeles detective, biblical apologetics expert, and a Fellow at the Colson Center for Christian Worldview, noted the tendency of people who reject God to nevertheless attempt to fashion substitutes more to their tastes. Wallace reflected on a trending downturn in Christian church attendance in the United States and Europe while atheists are starting "churches."

"Atheist churches have been formed across (the United States), apparently aiming to offer some features of a religious congregation," Wallace observed. Those features include "fellowship, collective enjoyment," and "a stimulus to moral behavior." The motto of an atheist church in Los Angeles is, "Live Better, Help Often, Wonder More."

J. Warner Wallace also noted that while increasing numbers of Americans and Europeans are moving away from institutional religion, they still hold on to ideas like "belief in the soul, divine energy," and "mystical realities." In fact, nine out of ten Americans believe in a higher power, even if it's not the God of the Bible, according to the Pew Research Center in a 2018 report.[118]

"We may just be innately religious," said Wallace.[119]

There is, then, good reason that God begins the Ten Commandments by declaring, "You shall have no other gods before Me." What we worship shapes us and our values. The critical issues in the age of artificial intelligence are these: What is the object of worship for the human makers of AI machines

---

[118] http://www.pewforum.org/2018/04/25/when-americans-say-they-believe-in-god-what-do-they-mean/

[119] Most Americans want some form of religious identity - Even atheists are creating churches | Fox News

some see as ultimately having god-like powers? What kind of deities have the developers manufactured in their own minds?

Professor Eric Ortlund wrote:

> The ancient idolater used half of a piece of wood to cook his food and then bowed low before the statue he carved from the other half; the modern idolater uses his laptop to pay bills, read the news … and possibly create a god.[120]

"New technologies kill old gods and give birth to new gods," said Juval Harari, an author and professor at Hebrew University of Jerusalem. That is why agricultural deities were different from hunter-gatherer spirits, why factory hands and peasants fantasized about different paradises, and why the revolutionary technologies of the 21st century are far more likely to spawn unprecedented religious movements than to revive medieval creeds."[121]

Harari sees the rise of more "techno-religion" in the future:

> Just as socialism took over the world by promising salvation through steam, so in the coming decades new techno-religions are likely to take over the world by promising salvation through algorithms and genes. In the 21st century we will create more powerful myths and more totalitarian religions than in any previous era. With the help of biotechnology and computer algorithms these religions will not only control our

---

[120] "AI Idolatry and the AI Singularity," By Eric Ortlund. Retrieved from http://oakhill2.ablette.net/blog/entry/idolatry_and_the_ai_singularity/, July 9, 2018.
[121] "Salvation By Algorithm," By Juval Harari. Retrieved from https://www.newstatesman.com/politics/uk/2016/09/salvation-algorithm-god-technology-and-new-21st-century-religions, July 9, 2018.

minute-by-minute existence, but will be able to shape our bodies, brains, and minds and to create entire virtual worlds, complete with hells and heavens.[122]

Decades ago, Jacques Ellul unwittingly gave a name to the new technical religion he could see emerging even then—"*technolatry.*"

A great quest in Arthur C. Clarke's *2001, a Space Odyssey* was for the spirit and soul of "HAL", the artificial intelligence computer that winds up playing god and judge with regard to the remaining humans aboard the Discovery 1 space-craft probing the universe. "HAL" stands for "heuristically programmed algorithmic computer."

A heuristic device is programmed to go to the solution of a problem as quickly as possible. This is done through short-cuts that may sacrifice degrees of accuracy to get to the best possible solution. HAL is sentient, meaning the AI machine is wired to have something resembling subjective feelings. This is fiction, though it represents a goal of artificial intelligence research.

MIT's Rosalind Picard has explored "affective computing", seeking ways to program machines to better understand human emotions, "We've decided it's more about building a better human-machine combination than it is about building a machine where we will be lucky if it wants us around as a household pet."[123]

Whether researchers recognize it or not the problem is the lack of *geist.*

---

[122] *Ibid.*

[123] Cited in John Lennox, 224, and at www.wired.co.uk/article/emotion-machines.

The German word *geist,* translated "spirit" or even "ghost," has metaphysical implications. The spirit of the human made in the Image of God has the functions of communion with God—conscience that can comprehend absolute, transcendent value as the standard for all ethics, and the ability to receive intuitions stirred in engagements with the Holy Spirit of God.

Spiritless AI can never be fully human, and yet there is a *geist,* a spirit that can exploit any material object that someone is willing to worship as a god (an idol). "An idol is nothing," writes St. Paul. "I am saying that these sacrifices (to idols) are offered to demons, not to God" (1 Corinthians 10:19-21; also see Deuteronomy 32:16-17).

Certainly, computers and artificial intelligence devices are not inherently demonic. However, to regard them consciously or unconsciously as gods is to open oneself to spiritual delusion. The idealistic naivete of scientism is dangerous because it dismisses the spiritual dimension, and in doing so, it makes itself vulnerable. Jacques Ellul did not live to see the emergence of artificial intelligence but was prophetic when he said,

> This world of the distraction or diversion or perversion of humanity by technology culminates in adoration, veneration, and beatification, in the expression of a properly religious sentiment. [...] As Marx showed, alienation leads to religion.[124]

The great quest of the demonic is for empty vessels they can fill. Jesus described it like this:

---

[124] Jacques Ellul, *The Technological Bluff,* translated by Geoffrey W. Bromiley (Grand Rapids: William B. Eerdmans Publishing Company), 382.

When an evil spirit leaves a person, it goes into the desert, seeking rest but finding none. Then it says, "I will return to the person I came from." So, it returns and finds its former home empty, swept, and in order. Then the spirit finds seven other spirits more evil than itself, and they all enter the person and live there. And so that person is worse off than before. That will be the experience of this evil generation.

(Matthew 12:43-45, NLT)

Clinical psychologist Adam J. Cox might not agree with everything here, but nevertheless, he frets about "the communication abilities of young males for whom a (technological) 'womb of all-encompassing stimulation' induces 'a pleasant trance from which they do not care to be awakened.'" Syndicated columnist George Will, himself an atheist, included Cox's quotes in a column. "We may yet rue the day we surrendered to the insistent urge to keep boredom at bay," wrote Will.[125]

Much has been written about the increase of demonization and the need for exorcists in our age. Many believe there is a link between demonic influence and control and the violence of our time. Humans with empty spirits are prime targets for demonization, but so are spiritless machines who become idols.

And people who take the Bible as actuality and not myth know there is another dark *geist* watching and waiting to exploit history and its events for global domination.

"Technological man will remold the world; he sees his task as Promethean and its stake as being and non-being," wrote

---

[125] "Lost in Electronica: The costs of 'the chaos of constant connection,'" By George Will, *Newsweek*, August 23 & 30, 2010, 22.

Romano Guardini, a twentieth-century German priest and academic described as one of "the most important figures in Catholic intellectual life in the 20th century."[126]

George Dyson was another of those modern deep thinkers. His primary area of interest was, in the description of Nicholas Carr, "the inner lives of machines." Dyson wrote a book, *Darwin Among the Machines.* Years after the release of the book, Dyson was thrilled to get an invitation to speak at the Googleplex, headquarters of Google—a dazzling temple among the modern god factories and a basilica of the religion of technolatry.

But Dyson's exhilaration turned to concern. The visit into the vast cyber temple and its efforts to develop artificial intelligence brought to Dyson's mind a paper authored by Alan Turing, the genius who led the project to break the Nazi Enigma code in the Second World War. In the monograph, Turing wrote, "We should not be irreverently usurping His power of creating souls, any more than we are in the procreation of children."

Dyson also recalled the report of a friend who had visited the Googleplex and observed happy people, dogs enjoying lawn sprinklers, and toys scattered throughout. Dyson's friend went on to say that despite all the gaiety, "I immediately suspected that unimaginable evil was happening somewhere in the dark corners. If the devil would come to earth, what place would be better to hide?"

Google cofounder Sergey Brin himself noted, "Some say Google is God," but others say, "Google is Satan."[127]

---

[126] Romano Guardini, *The End of the Modern World* (Intercollegiate Studies Institute, 2001) p.55.

[127] As cited in Carr, 174. Original source: George Dyson, "Turing's Cathedral

Both titles evoke the aura of great power. There is, however, a vast difference between the two—God has authority, but Satan has mere power. In this sense, authority is the transcendent right to hold and distribute power, while raw power is seized by those who do not have the ultimate right to it.

Therefore, the fundamental temptation in the fallen universe is power. "Nearly all men can stand adversity, but if you want to test a man's character, give him power," said an anonymous person reflecting on Abraham Lincoln.

Power draws the demonic like a sugary treat dropped on the ground on a hot summer day draws hordes of flies and ants. There is always a clustering of demons at centers of power. The Apostle John beheld a sweeping "unveiling" of the whole of history and interactions within it between the transcendent and immanent domains. The aged disciple wrote that he saw a vision in which a mighty, authoritative angel descended from heaven ...

> ... and the earth was lightened (illumed) with his glory. And he cried mightily with a strong voice, saying, Babylon the great is fallen, is fallen, and is become the habitation of devils, and the hold of every foul spirit, and a cage of every unclean and hateful bird. For all nations have drunk of the wine of the wrath of her fornication, and the kings of the earth have committed fornication with her, and the merchants of the earth are waxed rich through the abundance of her delicacies.[128]

I first became aware of this as a young man working in the White House. Sometimes I could feel a dark presence there.

---

[128] Revelation 18:1-3 (KJV). "Babylon" in the Revelation represents the world system without God and in willful denial of God.

At times, I passed it off as my emotions in the midst of the world's greatest center of human power. Later, however, Dr. Billy Graham privately told me he felt the same thing when he came to the White House (and later said this publicly).

It's not just the White House, but any seat of power, from the executive suite of a company to the leader of a family to the senior pastor or elder of a church, and all others. Historian and philosopher Baron Acton famously said, "Power corrupts, and absolute power corrupts absolutely. Great men are almost always bad men."

One interpreter of Acton's idea said, "As a person's power increases, their moral sense diminishes."[129]

Lucifer's essential temptation hurled at Adam and Eve was the enticement to take power over their own lives by disobeying God and eating the forbidden fruit. But the seduction of power goes back before the primeval sin of humanity. Isaiah 14 reveals that in pre-creation, Lucifer sought to displace God by elevating his own throne above all else.

Lucifer's primordial rebellion operates in the "spirit of Antichrist" which, as we discussed in Chapter Five, is already at work in the world, according to 1 John 4:3. Thus, the declaration of the godhood of AI is simply another of humanity's attempts to seize the throne of the Most High.

Anti, in Greek, not only means "against," as in English, but it also carries the idea of "in the place of." Therefore, the spirit of Antichrist is both opposition and imposition. He opposes Christ as the legitimate occupant of the throne of creation and desires to impose himself there. The Antichrist's aim is

---

[129] 'Absolute power corrupts absolutely' - who said it first? (phrases.org.uk)

opposition to Christ and imposition of himself on the throne rightfully occupied by Christ.

As we saw earlier, human beings made originally in the Image of God (*Imago Dei*) will even attempt to make creations in their own (fallen) image (*imago hominis*). Genesis says that God "breathed" into the form He had made, and it became a living "soul." What is it that human creators will breathe into the artificial intelligence machines they will construct? *Why would we build machines that become our lords and masters and jettison the true God of transcendent love and holiness?*

In the context of the godhood of artificial intelligence, Revelation 13 is especially haunting. Verse 15 says, "And it was given to him to give breath to the image of the beast, so that the image of the beast would even speak and cause as many as do not worship the image of the beast to be killed." Verse 18 provides the identity of the beast, identified by many interpreters as the Antichrist, "Here is wisdom. Let him who has understanding calculate the number of the beast, for the number is that of a man; and his number is six hundred and sixty-six."

The image of the beast is thus *imago hominis,* the image of "man."

Whether one views the Revelation passage as literal or not, it does present an ominous picture of power. It raises the question, in the worship of artificial intelligence as god, is it possible that humanity will become subject to an image that gains unprecedented power over the world and its people?

Are we building "666"?

CHAPTER 7

From Imago Dei to Imago Hominis

Just as the imago Dei was used to describe an analogy between humans and God, the imago hominis is that which establishes an analogy between humans and computers.

—Dr. Noreen L. Herzfeld[130]

On December 17, 2018, the *New York Times* published an essay by Clemson University philosophy professor Todd May that could signal an ominous turn for humanity.

"There are stirrings of discussion these days in philosophical circles about the prospects of human extinction," wrote Professor May. The question is "whether it would be a tragedy if the planet no longer contained human beings," the professor noted. Dr. May said that for him personally and tentatively "both that it would be a tragedy and that it might just be a good thing."[131]

---

[130] Noreen L. Herzfeld, *In Our Image: Artificial Intelligence and the Human Spirit* (Minneapolis: Fortress Press, 2002) 34.
[131] "Would Human Extinction Be a Tragedy?" by Todd May. Retrieved from https://www.nytimes.com/2018/12/17/opinion/human-extinction-climate-change.html, December 17, 2018.

How could the extinction of humanity be a good thing? How could one be so ambivalent about such a portent—even considering scholarly aloofness?

Though May was not writing from a theological perspective, one could conclude that the reason the removal of humanity from earth would be positive is because of the way people have abused the dominion mandate God gave to humans in the Garden of Eden:

> ... God created man in His own image, in the image of God created He him, and God said unto them, Be fruitful and multiply, and replenish the earth, and subdue it: and have dominion over the fish of the sea, and over the fowl of the air, and over every living thing that moveth upon the earth.   (Genesis 1:27-28 KJV)

That command was given to Adam and Eve prior to the fall into sin. They were to be the stewards of the world God had made, co-laborers with Him in its making, not exploiters and destroyers. However, God does not revoke His callings and giftings (Romans 11:29), and even though humanity chose evil, the command still stands. There can be no doubt that sinful, greedy men and women have abused nature.

"Human beings are destroying large parts of the inhabitable earth and causing unimaginable suffering to many of the animals that inhabit it," said May. "Humanity, then, is the source of devastation of the lives of conscious animals on a scale that is difficult to comprehend," the professor wrote.

But that might not be all bad, according to the discussions in philosophical circles regarding the extinction of at least those humans who will populate the future. "To demand of currently existing humans that they should end their lives would introduce significant suffering among those who have much to lose by dying." However, "Preventing future humans from existing does not introduce such suffering, since those human beings will not exist and therefore not have lives to sacrifice."

The fact that such conclusions could be the outcome of serious discussion is shocking. However, it reveals something of the philosophical atmosphere in which AI is developing.

Such philosophy is drastically without any view of transcendence. Nevertheless, it quests for an ethic. "It may well be, then, that the extinction of humanity would make the world better off and yet would be a tragedy," wrote May, but without a transcendent perspective, the professor can only be ambivalent. "I don't want to say this for sure, [...] but it certainly seems a live possibility [that the world would be better without humans], and that by itself disturbs me."

One solution from another quarter without reference to transcendence would be the radical alteration of human beings by making them more like machines. The discussion in philosophical circles might even lead to a formalized ethic that would support the gradual extinction of humanity through engineering transhumans who are increasingly more like AI robots than humans. The day might come when the humanity will have been totally displaced by the mechanical.

Is this discussion that wonders about the ethics and benefits of the extinction of humanity the beginning of a possible convergence of non-transcendence philosophy and non-transcendence scientism?

Perhaps the Saudi Arabians have given us a peek at what may be ahead. On October 25, 2017, the Kingdom granted citizenship to a non-human. "Sophia" had a feminine name and certain functional capacities that all humans possess, but Sophia was a robot programmed with artificial intelligence. The citizenship was bestowed at a conference in Riyadh, where Sophia's maker, Hanson Robotics, displayed its highly advanced technology.

The implications went beyond the technological, bringing into stark awareness a vital question in the cyborg age: *What is a human being?*

Raw materialism, absent any sense of the transcendent, would hold that granting citizenship to a robot "makes sense," wrote biochemist Fazale Rana. In the "intellectual framework" of materialism "human beings are largely regarded as biological machines, and the brain as an organic computer," said Rana. "If AI systems can be created with self-awareness and emotional capacity, what make them any different from human beings?"

At the same time, granting the robot citizenship "establishes a dangerous precedent," Rana thought. It could be "a harbinger to a dystopian future where machines (and animals with enhanced intelligence) are afforded the same rights as human beings." This "threatens to undermine human dignity and worth and, along with it, the biblical conception of humanity," Rana said.[132]

The question, therefore, is not only what a human being is, but how does a person with a brain that some regard as an organic computer differ from a human-made machine that

---

[132] "Does Development of Artificial Intelligence Undermine Human Exceptionalism?" by Fazale Rana. Retrieved from https://www.twr360.org/blog/details/1839/does-development-of-artificial-intelligence-undermine-human-exceptionalism, November 29, 2018.

has self-awareness and sentience enabled by a silicon-based "brain"?

Ecclesiastes 3:11 gives a striking answer. God has placed *eternity* in the human heart or spirit. Literally, the Hebrew word means the capacity to see beyond the present moment all the way to the vanishing point. The person, made in the image of God, has an innate sense of something beyond finite time and space—infinity, a transcendent reality. The creators of *imago hominis* cannot wire or program that abstract awareness into the AI machine. The engineers can put information about the fact that humans can sense the transcendent-beyond, but not the sense itself.

As we noted earlier, the machine lacks a *geist*, a spirit, and therefore cannot grasp things spiritually discerned—like biblical revelation and the presence and work of the Holy Spirit in the human spirit.

Biochemist Rana believes that AI systems don't have actual self-awareness and never will, though they "are on a steep trajectory toward ever-increasing sophistication." In reality, he says, "those systems are becoming better and better at *mimicking* human cognitive abilities, emotions, and even self-awareness." As Rana sees it, AI systems "do not inherently possess these capabilities—and I don't think they ever will."[133]

Ultimately, the question might not be whether we will make AI computers in the human image, but whether the computers will make us in their image. Joseph Weizenbaum says,

> The great danger we face as we become more intimately involved with our computers—as we come to

---

[133] *Ibid.* Italics in original.

experience more of our lives through the disembodied symbols flickering across our screens—is that we will begin to lose our humanness, to sacrifice the very qualities that separate us from machines."[134]

What a dizzying reduction—from the image of God to the image of the machine!

"Everything that human beings are doing to make it easier to operate computer networks is at the same time, but for different reasons, making it easier for computer networks to operate human beings," wrote George Dyson, author of *Darwin Among the Machines.*[135]

Both Friedrich Nietzsche in the nineteenth century and T.S. Eliot in the twentieth awoke to this stark awareness. Nietzsche watched the printing ball on his early typewriter and felt that it was "a thing like me." Worse, he feared he was becoming "a thing like it," and that it was actually forming his thoughts. In 1916, T.S. Eliot wrote a friend that when he composed on the typewriter, "I find that I am sloughing off all my long sentences which I used to dote upon."[136]

That God made man and woman in His image is the highest possible view of the human, and it is grasped only in the context of transcendence.

Historian Robin Jensen, in writing about the development of Christian art, says, "Through the grandeur and beauty of the creatures we may, by analogy, contemplate their Author."

---

[134] Nicholas Carr, *The Shallows: What the Internet Is Doing to Our Brains* (New York: W.W. Norton & Company, 2010), 207.
[135] George B. Dyson, *Darwin Among the Machines: The Evolution of Global Intelligence* (Reading, MA: Addison-Wesley, 1977), 10. Cited in Carr, 173-174.
[136] Carr, 209.

This, writes Glen W. Olsen, "is the ground of a Christian understanding of transcendence."[137]

When God created people in His image, He made man and woman as triune beings like Himself. The Holy Trinity is Father, Son, and Holy Spirit. The human being is spirit, soul, and body (1 Thessalonians 5:23). The new AI gods will have a mechanical body and a cyber-mind, but as I said, they will be spiritless. They will have no sense of the transcendent. Thus, their moral and ethical decisions will be made without reference to anything above and beyond themselves—ominously, including their makers.

Michael Engor, professor of neurological surgery at Stony Brook University, has spent a career studying the human brain and mind and writes:

> Materialism, the view that matter is all that exists, is the premise of much contemporary thinking about what a human is. Yet evidence from the laboratory, operating room, and clinical experience points to a less fashionable conclusion: Humans straddle the material and *immaterial* realms (italics added).

Better science and medicine, Engor says, will come "when we recognize that human beings have abilities that transcend reductionist material explanations."[138]

Research psychologist Robert Epstein demolishes the reductionist argument. Epstein notes David Hart's quip that "young materialists" dream of growing up to be a computer.

---

[137] Glen W. Olsen, *The Turn to Transcendence: The Role of Religion in the Twenty-First Century* (Catholic University Press, 2010), 162.
[138] "A Map of the Soul," by Michael Engor, M.D. Retrieved from https://www.firstthings.com/web-exclusives/2017/06/a-map-of-the-soul, December 4, 2018.

But the fact is, men and women are humans, not computers, says Epstein. Computers are machines that store information in contrast to the brain that does not merely provide storage space for data, but changes when we have learned a song we can sing or recite a poem. "When called on to perform, neither the song nor the poem is any sense 'retrieved' from anywhere in the brain. [...] We simple sing or recite—no retrieval necessary."[139]

This points to the fact that the human being, through the spirit, has the capacity to commune with transcendent Being—God. "The bodies of organisms are organized as it were pneumatically, from within, infused throughout by the Spirit of life, which is personal, intentional, artistic, and creative," writes Anthony Esolen, who reminds us of the Psalm, "You send forth Your Spirit, and they are created."[140]

The contradiction, in light of Levandowski and others, is the AI machine humans may worship will be without a spirit. Missing will be the capacities of communion with God, conscience that reaches beyond the relativity of value, ethics, and morality, and the ability to receive the intuitions of the Holy Spirit, all of which manifest through the Holy Spirit's interaction with the human spirit.

The big problem in distinguishing between good and bad, says philosopher Simon Blackburn, "is one of finding room for ethics, or of placing ethics within the disenchanted, non-ethical order which we inhabit, and of which we are a part."[141]

---

[139] "Is the Human Brain Just Like a Computer?" by Anthony Esolen. Retrieved from https://theimaginativeconservative.org/2018/07/how-brain-not-like-computer-anthony-esolen.html, December 4, 2018.
[140] *Ibid.*
[141] Quoted in Berlinski, 35.

"The impulse of our century has been to substitute earth for God as an object of reverence," says Louis Gluck. He continues,

> But the religious mind, with its hunger for meaning and disposition to awe, its craving for the path, the continuum, the unbroken line, for what is final, immutable, cannot sustain itself on matter and natural process.[142]

Such is the nature of spirit, but how does one program a non-material spirit in a machine? What is the algorithm of spirit?

The human spirit is often represented in the Bible as the heart of the person—especially in the Old Testament. There the view is not optimistic, and the human needs transformation. "The heart is more deceitful than all else and is desperately sick," wrote the Prophet Jeremiah (Jeremiah 17:9). Jesus says in the New Testament that "out of the heart come evil thoughts, adulteries, fornications, thefts, false witness, slanders [...] the things that defile the man" (Matthew 15:19).

For good reason, C.S. Lewis warned about "the atrophy of the chest." "Reason in man must rule the mere appetites by means of the spiritual element," wrote Lewis. "The head rules the belly through the chest—the seat of magnanimity, of emotions organized by trained habit into stable sentiments." In fact, "it is by this middle element that man is man, for by his intellect he is mere spirit and by his appetite mere animal."[143]

---

[142] Quoted in Olsen, 1.

[143] C.S. Lewis, *The Abolition of Man* (New York: HarperCollins, 1974), 25-26.

Secularists may not agree with the Bible's assessment of human nature nor the concern of C.S. Lewis about "chestlessness", but even they sense something is wrong and that transformation is needed. In an analysis titled, "C.S. Lewis and the Advent of the Posthuman," James a Herrick cites the thought of Professor Julian Savelescu, who leads Oxford University's Center for Practical Ethics. "He is," writes Herrick, "a leading proponent of human enhancement." In Herrick's description, Savulescu is concerned that "deep moral flaws and destructive behaviors point indisputably to the need to employ technology and education to change human nature." Otherwise, the human species may become extinct.[144]

Savelescu contemplates human nature in the context of technological advance, and his palms are sweaty. Even though he and his intellectual compatriots may not believe in original sin, he nevertheless feels the urgency to promote "certain sets of values" and engage in "moral education." Individuals in the new world of the coming gods "will need to accept an ethics of restraint."

Savulescu frets about all this because "liberal democracy" is not supportive of "any particular set of values or particular moral education," but seeks only "maximum freedom." Savelescu has to face the hard fact, "We have a human nature that is severely limited in terms of its origins and in terms of its capacity to respond to these new challenges."[145]

The great peril is that it is such "severely limited" humans who are building machines in their own image. As the robots can expand on the knowledge base given to them and go beyond humans, will they also expand on the moral codes—or lack

---

[144] *The Magician's Twin: C.S. Lewis on Science, Scientism, and Society,* Edited by John G. West (Seattle: Discovery Institute Press, 2012) 235.
[145] *Ibid.,* 236.

thereof—programmed into them (or not) by humans who need transformation but deny the transcendent Source that is essential for true transformation?

C.S. Lewis saw that transcendent value in the *Tao,* "a timeless and universal expression of value reflecting the moral nature of God Himself."[146] Lewis saw the danger in science attempting to redesign the human and to do so "operating outside the limits" of the *Tao.*[147]

Stuart Russell is a research advisor at the Machine Intelligence Research Institute (MIRI). He says a goal of artificial intelligence research and development "is to make better decision-making systems." But, Stuart says, "to build a super-intelligent machine, you have to give it something that you want it to do." This raises the danger that you give it something that isn't "actually what you want." This might happen "if you're not really good at expressing what you really want, *or even knowing what you really want* (emphasis added)—until it's too late and you see you don't like it."[148]

The HAL computer, the fictitious machine in Arthur Clarke's *2001: A Space Odyssey,* was only doing what it was told to do. Of course, HAL had taken the original instruction of its makers beyond what they intended, but the machine threatening human life on the spacecraft had built on the foundational algorithms embedded by other humans. HAL was *imago hominis,* in the image of humans. The men and women who exulted in their achievement had never intended for HAL to try to become a god, holding the lives and deaths of other people in its circuitry.

---

[146] *Ibid.,* 244.

[147] *Ibid.,* 238.

[148] About the Machine Intelligence Research Institute

Perhaps they had never read Mary Shelley, the literary creator of Frankenstein. In the tale, she described a chilling moment when the monster created by Dr. Frankenstein awakens to who he is in contrast to humans. The creature's prime goal, writes Shelley, becomes that of reducing "his creator to the same state of isolation that he must endure."[149]

This prompts a crucial question: *Do we as humans really want to see ourselves as part or even wholly as machines?* C.S. Lewis puts it bluntly when he writes that,

> Either we are rational spirit obliged for ever to obey the absolute values of the *Tao,* or else we are mere nature to be kneaded and cut into new shapes for the pleasures of masters who must, by hypothesis, have no motive but their own "natural" impulses.[150]

Stuart Russell is more optimistic and likes to think about artificial intelligence "in terms of an optimization problem." Seen that way, the AI device:

> … is solving an optimization problem for you, and you leave out some of the variables that you actually care about. [...] It's in the nature of optimization problems that if the system gets to manipulate some variables that don't form part of the objective function—so it's free to play with those as much as it wants—often, in order to optimize the ones that it is supposed to optimize, it will set the other ones to extreme values.[151]

---

[149] Mary Shelley, *Frankenstein* (New York: Tom Doherty Associates, 1988), 235.
[150] C.S. Lewis, *The Abolition of Man* (New York: HarperCollins Publishers, 1974), 73.
[151] Stuart Russell, "The Long-Term Future of Artificial Intelligence," Retrieved from https://intelligence.org/about/, July 12, 2018.

Increasingly, those who envision *Imago Dei* making *imago hominis* no longer see a bare machine but a joining of the human being and the machine, resulting in the *transhuman.* Oxford philosopher Nick Bostrom is a founder of transhumanism. He characterizes it like this:

> Transhumanists view human nature as a work-in-progress, a half-baked beginning that we can remold in desirable ways. Current humanity need not be the endpoint of evolution. Transhumanists hope that by responsible use of science, technology, and other rational means, we shall eventually manage to become post-human, beings with vastly greater capacities than present human beings have.[152]

Such a movement and its inventions may become inevitable, given the nature of science—*if it can be done, it will be done.* When the transhumans begin to appear, humanity will indeed have reached a new epoch, one increasingly severed from antiquity and the classic understanding of the human. Civilization rests on the ancient concept of the human being made in the image of God. It is this concept that is presupposed in the founding documents of free nations. The American Declaration of Independence, for example, states that "all men [people] are *created* equal, they are *endowed* by their Creator with certain inalienable rights, that among these are life, liberty and the pursuit of happiness" (italics added).

If we think of the AI machine made by humans, we must ask, *What value and what inalienable rights will ad hominis build into the machine?* The question becomes more complex when we apply the worldview stated in the Declaration of

---

[152] "Transhumanist Values," by Nick Bostrom, April 18, 2001. Retrieved from https://nickbostrom.com/ethics/values.html, November 28, 2018. Also cited in West, *et al.,* 251.

Independence to a mechanism that is part human and part machine.

"Man's conquest of himself means simply the rule of the Conditioners over the Conditioned human material, the world of *post-humanity,*" writes Paul Gosselin. Some people "knowingly and some unknowingly" are "laboring to produce" this coming world, he says.[153]

Mortimer Adler shows the historic view of the nature of the human being as *imago Dei* on which civilization rests; he writes that "four Christian cosmological presuppositions [...] formed the basis for the traditional Western perspective on man:

1. **The dogma of personality** – Man alone is made in the image of God. He is distinguished from animals by possessing a soul.
2. **The dogma of the special creation of man** – Man cannot be explained solely in terms of natural causes.
3. **The dogma of individual mortality** – It is postulated that after death, the human soul is able to exist without the body and will be reunited with a recreated body at the resurrection.
4. **The dogma of free will and moral responsibility** – This implies that man must answer to divine law and is free in his choices, able to distinguish between good and evil.[154]

Which of these attributes will the human grant to the machine? Will *ad hominis* be capable of a loving relationship with its creator as *imago Dei* has with his or hers? In the transhuman, how will the attributes be divided? Will the human

---

[153] Gosselin, Vol. 1, 228.

[154] Paul Gosselin, *Flight From the Absolute: Cynical Observations on the Postmodern West,* Vol. I (Quebec: Samizdat), 218.

side become immortal through the uploading of its brain into the memory of the machine?

The danger—and sadness—is that the AI device will always be sub-human to one degree or another and therefore not human at all.

"GHASTLY SIMPLICITY"

C.S. Lewis may never have imagined artificial intelligence, though he had a striking understanding of the ethos in which it is rising. As we discussed earlier, in *The Abolition of Man,* he spoke of "men without chests" in the sense of the heartlessness of people without God and awareness of the transcendent. "In a sort of ghastly simplicity, we remove the organ and demand the function. We make men without chests and expect of them virtue and enterprise. We laugh at honour and are shocked to find traitors in our midst."[155]

Will spiritless AI robots "without chests" ultimately be traitors against the very humans who build them as humans themselves have turned away from God in His transcendence?

Bradley J. Birzer reflects on *The Abolition of Man* 75 years after C.S. Lewis penned it. He concludes that "the scientists and technologists and state makers and educational institutions and corporations have not ignored Lewis' *Abolition of Man*" [...] but "have continued on the deadly path of making man not in the image of God, as manifested in nature, but in the image of some men, as manipulated by nature."[156]

---

[155] C.S. Lewis, *The Abolition of Man* (New York: Touchstone, 1996), 35-37.
[156] "Progressing Toward What? C.S. Lewis & 'The Abolition of Man,'" by Bradley J. Birzer, *The Imaginative Conservative*, August 8, 2018. Retrieved from https://theimaginativeconservative.org/2018/08/progressing-toward-what-c-s-lewis-abolition-of-man-bradley-birzer.html.

Thus, Lewis was concerned about the coming of the "man-moulders (*sic.*) of the new age" who would be "armed with the powers of an omnicompetent state and an irresistible scientific technique." Under these powerful "man-moulders," Lewis warned that "we shall get a race of conditioners who really can cut out all posterity in any shape they please."[157]

Acknowledged or not, the rise of the "conditioners" must be a major concern in the age of artificial intelligence. They will become not only shapers of human nature, but religious police, enforcing the worship of the AI idol. Such adulation may be the consummate attempt to displace the transcendent God by trying to push Him off His throne.

It has been tried before, and the outcome is always catastrophic.

---

[157] C.S. Lewis, *The Abolition of Man* (New York: Macmillan, 1947), 36.

CHAPTER 8

The View from the "Valley"

Major Worldviews of AI Philosophy

Many residents of Silicon Valley harbor bizarre worldviews.
—Noah Baron[158]

How do the people who are developing and programming the gods of the future see the world? How can principle get into the logic systems of an AI machine? And what principles would the programmers install? What are the spiritual, philosophical, ethical, and moral beliefs that humans will wire into *imago hominis,* and how will they do it?

What are the "permanent things" (to borrow Russell Kirk's terminology) that will be constants in the AI machine, meaning that no matter where their self-learning takes them, these constants will be immovable like the "ancient boundaries" set by the "fathers" in Proverbs 22:28?

---

[158] "Silicon Valley's Poverty of Philosophy," By Noah Baron. https://www.huffingtonpost.com/entry/silicon-valleys-poverty-of-philosophy_us_59792e64e4b0c69ef7052571

Russell Kirk reminds us that by "the Permanent Things," T. S. Eliot "meant those elements in the human condition that give us our nature, without which we are as the beasts that perish. They work upon us all in the sense that both they and we are bound up in that continuity of belief and institution called the great mysterious incorporation of the human race."[159]

These are all vital worldview issues. They can be answered only by understanding the worldview of AI makers that gets programmed into the machines.

Steve Jobs may have been reflecting an important component of the Silicon worldview when he contemplated death, "I'm about fifty-fifty on believing in God. [...] For most of my life I've felt there must be something more to existence than meets the eye."

Facing death from pancreatic cancer, Jobs seemed to have been giving evidence of *ambiguity* as a major component in his worldview relating to transcendence and perhaps in the worldview of many others in Silicon Valley.

At one point in his musings about dying, Jobs said that he liked "to think that something survives after you die. [...] But on the other hand, perhaps it's like an on-off switch: Click! And you're gone. Maybe that's why I never liked to put on-off switches on Apple devices."[160]

A worldview afloat on ambiguity has significant implications regarding decision-making and values. However, despite Job's preference, non-ambiguous on-off switches for artificial

---

[159] "The Permanent Things," By Russell Kirk, *The Imaginative Conservative,* February 9, 2013, The Permanent Things - The Imaginative Conservative.
[160] Walter Isaacson, *Steve Jobs* (New York: Simon and Schuster, 2011), 570-571.

intelligence devices are essential. A question of apocalyptic proportions may loom in the future as a desperate humanity asks, *How can we stop these machines?* There will be no room for philosophical haziness regarding such a conundrum.

That brings us back to the fundamental question of this book, *Who will rule the coming gods?* What do the people who program limits into AI devices believe ethically, morally, and spiritually? On-off switches deal with absolutes. What are the absolute values that set boundaries on beliefs for the tech titans and their minions and behavior embedded in their worldviews individually and collectively?

How do the creators of the machines see the world?

All worldviews are religious in the sense that they seek to answer ultimate questions and rest on values. James Sire lists eight essential questions every worldview should answer:[161]

1. What is ultimate reality?
2. What is the nature of external reality? The world around us?
3. What is a human being?
4. What happens to a person at death?
5. Why is it possible to know anything at all?
6. How do we know what is right and wrong?
7. What is the meaning of human history?
8. What personal, life-orienting commitments are consistent with this worldview?

To explore each of these in relation to AI would require another entire book. However, the question at the heart of

---

[161] https://www.christianity.com/theology/other-religions-beliefs/8-questions-every-worldview-must-answer.html

the issue of transcendence is Sire's first one, *What is ultimate reality?*

Answering the question requires going back in history to the Enlightenment and the reach of its tentacles into modern time. Fazale R. Rana and Kenneth R. Samples write, "In some respects transhumanism, the merger of humans and AI machines, is the culmination of the vision of the Enlightenment, a philosophical movement of the seventeenth and eighteenth centuries."[162] The movement that Western culture embraced saw reason as the ultimate, "the only legitimate authority."[163]

Rana and Samples quote Rene Descartes, the seventeenth-century French philosopher who many regard as the father of philosophy, when he said that humanity might come to the point in its acquisition of knowledge of the natural world when humans might "thereby make ourselves, as it were, the lords and masters of nature."[164]

In contemporary times, Ben Saunders says that "techno-faith" is "a fundamental belief in the power of the human will to transform the world to reflect human desires, through the agency of technology."[165]

In this worldview, humans, their self-interests, and capacities for reason constitute the ultimate reality in the minds of many creators of the tech-world—for which Silicon Valley and its concentration of companies is a prime symbol.

---

[162] Fazale R. Rana and Kenneth R. Samples, *Humans 2.0: Scientific, Philosophical, and Theological Perspectives on Transhumanism* (Covina, CA., RTB Press, 2019), 19.
[163] *Ibid.*
[164] *Ibid.*
[165] *Ibid.*

However, Silicon Valley is not godless, and neither is the tech-world. Skip Vaccarello has lived in Silicon Valley, the heart of America's tech world, for more than 40 years. In his book, *Finding God in Silicon Valley,* he breaks through common assumptions regarding its secularity.

Vaccarello writes on his website, "It may surprise you that the God of the Bible is active and working in Silicon Valley. He is at the center of the lives of many entrepreneurs, venture capitalists, business and non-profit leaders, programmers, and ordinary people."[166]

It is crucial to know the core elements of what we will call here the "Silicon Valley Worldview" for three reasons:

First, as artificial intelligence development reaches toward producing a machine with some level of consciousness, the makers will unwittingly program their own worldviews into the machines.

Second, worldviews evolve value systems, and therefore, the principles inherent in the worldviews of the human developers will be the values that determine algorithms and set boundaries for the actions of the artificial intelligence robots.

Frank Pasquale writes in his book, *The Black Box Society: The Secret Algorithms that Control Money and Information,* "Proprietary algorithms [...] are immune from scrutiny." They render us vulnerable to surveillance, censorship masking as persuasion, and so "undermining the openness of our society." Almost all "the major social media networks" promote the worldviews associated with progressivism and "left-wing politics." Because of "the monopolistic power" of

---

[166] Finding God in Silicon Valley

the big networks, "contamination" with such worldviews "is inevitable."[167]

Third, censorship is an increasing concern, and the Silicon Valley worldview will set the criteria by which such censorship works. Facebook CEO Mark Zuckerberg told a congressional committee in 2018 that he understood the concern because his huge company and the tech industry in general are head-quartered in California's Silicon Valley, which he described as *"an extremely left-leaning place."*[168]

If the time comes that artificial intelligence dictates thought to an increasingly compliant humanity, what will be the philosophies that determine what people can know and express?

The answer to that is in the details of the philosophy. What, then, are the key components of the Silicon Valley worldview that determine how many makers of artificial intelligence devices will answer life's most important questions?

Carl Cantana, a former Google software engineer living in San Francisco, reflects on the Silicon Valley culture he experienced and states these characteristics:

- **Self-Righteousness** – "Very few people seem comfortable admitting that maybe, just possibly, they are not changing the world. Many people have a savior complex, even if they are working on a food delivery app. It's unlike anything I've seen anywhere else. At

---

[167] "Silicon Valley's Futile Search for Utopia Via the 'Perfect Algorithm'", by David Solway, September 13, 2018. Retrieved from https://pjmedia.com/trending/silicon-valleys-futile-search-for-utopia-via-the-perfect-algorithm/

[168] https://townhall.com/columnists/jerrynewcombe/2018/05/31/shall-the-geeks-inherit-the-earth-n2485908, italics added.

least in New York, people feel comfortable admitting they're in it for the money," says Cantana.[169]

- **Hedonistic Subculture** – Organizational psychologist Barbara Adams says there is a difference between the "espoused values" of Silicon values and the actual "values-in-use." The actuality, she writes, suggests "burnout from a killer work culture, rampant sexism and ageism, embarrassing lack of ethnic, racial, and gender diversity, and a perverse pride in lack of professionalism."[170]

- **Utilitarianism** – Utilitarianism believes that things are right and good if they have practical outcomes for the majority of people. It is a primary doctrine promoting the idea that the ends justify the means. Noah Baron, the civil rights attorney quoted at the beginning of this chapter, told of going to a party not long after he moved to San Francisco. Most of the attendees were from the Silicon Valley tech industry. In a conversation with one of them, the man argued that (Communist) China's single-party system was better than American democracy because it's "more efficient." Baron responded that though the American system has its imperfections, it nevertheless "preserves many of our political freedoms and secures rights of workers to an extent unknown in China." The Silicon Valley man could only reply by noting China's "massive" economic growth.[171]

- **Objectivism** – "Perhaps the most influential figure in the (tech) industry [...] isn't Steve Jobs or Sheryl Sandberg, but rather Ayn Rand," according to an

---

[169] Is Silicon Valley culture hedonistic? - Quora Is Silicon Valley culture hedonistic? - Quora
[170] *Ibid.*
[171] https://www.huffingtonpost.com/entry/silicon-valleys-poverty-of-philosophy_us_59792e64e4b0c69ef7052571

article in *Vanity Fair*. "At their core, Rand's philosophies suggest that it's O.K. to be selfish, greedy, and self-interested, especially in business, and that a win-at-all-costs mentality is just the price of changing the norms of society." Someone said that Rand's books should be retitled, "It's O.K. to Be a Sociopath."[172] Rand promoted objectivism, the idea that what matters is what exists in the existential world rather than the transcendent. Knowledge comes by reason, not revelation. The highest moral goal for any individual is his or her own happiness.

- **Progressivism** – "The French Revolution, communism, and Nazism each believed itself the vanguard of a dawning age. They each claimed a position for their version of the *new man* (in original), gloriously evolved individuals who had glimpsed into the very cosmic truth of where history was marching," writes Peter M. Burfeind.[173] Many in Silicon Valley believe they are on the leading edge of the "right side" of history and will bring into reality the technology that will be messianic in saving people and the world they inhabit from the "hell" of the old world and its cumbersome values. The "new transhuman" is the dream of the makers of artificial intelligence.

Writing in the *New York Times,* Farhad Manjoo summed up the Silicon Valley worldview:

A 2017 Stanford University survey of Silicon Valley elites sought to discover the principles that would guide policy as they and their industries grow as a political force. The findings provide a clear summation

---

[172] https://www.vanityfair.com/news/2016/10/silicon-valley-ayn-rand-obsession
[173] Burfeind, *Gnostic America,* 53.

of the Silicon Valley worldview, especially as it relates to political philosophy. The study showed that tech entrepreneurs are very liberal—among some of the most left-leaning Democrats you can find. They are overwhelmingly in favor of economic policies that redistribute wealth, including higher taxes on rich people and lots of social services for the poor, including universal health care. Their outlook is cosmopolitan and globalist—they support free trade and more open immigration, and they score low on measures of "racial resentment. [...] They oppose restrictions on abortion, favor gay rights, support gun control, and oppose the death penalty.

The Stanford survey showed one area where the leaders of Silicon Valley "deviate from Democratic orthodoxy." They don't like "government's efforts to regulate business, especially when it comes to labor."[174]

Worldviews arise from religious beliefs. Such systems try to answer the questions of deity and ultimacy. What or who is supreme in the universe? What or who caused creation? What is the position of the reasoning, feeling human being with respect to the ultimate? What is the purpose of it all?

Israeli academician and writer Juval Harari sensed the religious vibes in the AI cosmos. "If you want to meet the prophets who will be remaking the 21st century, don't bother going to the Arabian Desert or the Jordan Valley—go to Silicon Valley," Harari said.[175]

---

[174] "Silicon Valley's Politics: Liberal, With One Big Exception," By Farhad Manjoo, September 6, 2017. Retrieved from https://www.nytimes.com/2017/09/06/technology/silicon-valley-politics.html

[175] https://www.newstatesman.com/politics/uk/2016/09/salvation-algorithm-god-technology-and-new-21st-century-religions

But those prophets are not proclaiming a biblical message. "You can be openly polyamorous, and people will call you brave. You can put micro-doses of LSD in your cereal, and people will call you a pioneer. But the one thing you cannot be is a Christian." So said a participant appearing in HBO's *Silicon Valley*, referring to the religious atmosphere of the region and the realm of which it is the capital. Silicon Valley is "statistically one of the least religious sections of the states, with sixty-one percent of the Bay Area [of California] not attending church, compared to a thirty-eight percent average," wrote Zara Stone in a *Forbes* report.[176]

But again, that does not mean that the heart of computerdom is without religion. Silicon Valley does believe that something—if not Someone—is ultimate, and like all religious people, its adherents interpret the world through the lens of that belief system. It may not be compatible with Christianity, but Silicon Valley religion is as doctrinaire as any church or denomination.

Worldviews produce doctrinal systems, whether theistic or not. The AI religion, though it may have been created by fun-loving freethinkers, is nevertheless developing its own magisterium, sets of dogma that would vie with stacks of systematic theologies, except this dogma centers on AI-ology.

Jesus Christ shared with His people a grand vision for the coming of the Kingdom of God into the world—the Kingdom of righteousness, peace, and joy in the Holy Spirit (Matthew 24; Romans 14:17). Levandowski also has a kingdom vision:

---

[176] "How a Spirituality Startup Is Solving Silicon Valley's Religious Apathy," by Zara Stone, *Forbes*, April 26, 2018. Retrieved from https://www.forbes.com/sites/zarastone/2018/04/26/how-a-spirituality-startups-solving-silicon-valleys-religious-apathy/#6eccbf452ed9, November 28, 2018.

*Way of the Future is about creating a peaceful
and respectful transition of who is in charge of the planet
from people to people + machines.*[177]

AI religion's god is strictly quantitative. What qualifies the machine as being godlike is that it possesses more *quanta* than mere humans. "It's not a god in the sense that it makes lightning or causes hurricanes," Levandowski says. "But if there is something a billion times smarter than the smartest human, what else are you going to call it?"[178]

Yet as we have seen elsewhere in this book, the true and transcendent God cannot be created because He is eternally "I Am"—not "I was" or "I will be." He interacts with finite time, but He is not *in* time, bound to finitude.

God's omniscience is not merely a greater collection of data than that held by humans, but knowledge of the *essence* of all things. That is, in His transcendent mind, God knows the actuality of pure Being. By contrast, the human on the immanent plane sees only the manifestation of phenomena in time and space and knows appearance and function to which he or she gives a name. To put it another way, a person may know the name of someone or something, but God knows what's behind the name, essence, or essential being of the person.

Isaiah 42:20 reveals the limitations of human vision without transcendence, "You [humans] have seen many things, but you do not observe them." Thus, "God sees not as man sees, for man looks at the outward appearance, but the LORD looks at the heart" (1 Samuel 16:7).

---

[177] Inside "Way Of The Future": A Religious Organization For Machines (analyticsindiamag.com)
[178] https://www.cnet.com/news/the-new-church-of-ai-god-is-even-creepier-than-i-imagined/

The God revealed in the Bible is the Spirit in whom "spirit and truth" combine (John 4). "Spirit" refers to His qualitative Being of otherness, while "truth" is the objective information He knows—which is all information about all things.

Humans have invested the word "spirit" with all kinds of meanings, from the ethereal to the ghostly. The old translators of the Bible into English even called the Holy Spirit the Holy "Ghost." But authentic spirit has to do with dimensionality and otherness.

Levandowski and his AI religion probably don't represent the major view in Silicon Valley. However, Levandowski is one of the Silicon Valley inhabitants who believes artificial intelligence will transform human existence and even dictate "whether our species survives or not."[179]

The AI religious view of God *is immanence pretending to transcendence.* This belief is dangerous to its adherents. History shows what happens when people ascribe transcendence to institutions and individuals who actually exist on the immanent scale. When humans structure their own deities, they easily become instruments of exploitation.

Despite all this, AI religion shares with Christianity a theology of *soteriology* or salvation. This means there is evil from which the world must be saved.

---

[179] http://www.dailymail.co.uk/sciencetech/article-5088473/Founder-church-AI-says-raising-god.html

- Sin and evil

"Google professed a sense of moral purity—as exemplified by its informal motto, 'Don't be evil.'"[180] That slogan has now been changed to "do the right thing"—but what is the right thing according to Google and others especially working in developing artificial intelligence? The right thing in Google's eyes is the moral thing. However, "moral" seems to be thoroughly pragmatic or in the eye of the beholder in the AI catechism. If this characterizes AI religion, then it is another form of legalism. However, grace is needed in computerdom, and without it, all that's left is a do-or-die progressivism.

Yuval Noah Harari reflects on the emergence of AI religion and its promised salvation and sees it in the context of Marx:

> The socialists created a brave new religion for a brave new world. They promised salvation through technology and economics, thus establishing the first techno-religion in history and changing the foundations of human discourse. Up until then, the great religious debates revolved around gods, souls, and the afterlife. [...] After Marx, however, questions of technology and economic production became far more divisive and important than questions about the soul and the afterlife.[181]

Progressivism is not only a worldview but a religion for many. Not only is the doctrine of the coming kingdom important in Judaism and Christianity, but also in AI religion, as we have seen. The AI tech world is full of congregants who pursue a

---

[180] Stephen Levy, *In the Plex: How Google Thinks, Works, and Shapes Our Lives* (New York: Simon and Schuster, 2011) 6.
[181] Harari, https://www.newstatesman.com/politics/uk/2016/09/salvation-algorithm-god-technology-and-new-21st-century-religions

kingdom vision, one in which human-made superintelligence plays an angelic role in the sense of Hebrews 1:14 which says that God sent them as "ministering spirits" to render service for the sake of "those who will inherit salvation."

"Progressives believe they have unique insight, a secret *gnosis* [knowledge] into the cosmic end toward which society must *progress,* and their cosmically-ordained task is to lead their benighted fellow citizens toward this end," says Peter Burfeind.[182]

AI religion even displays evangelistic zeal and missionary vision. Google co-founder Larry Page had a vision from childhood of transforming the world. He wanted to be an inventor because, as he said, "I really wanted to change the world. [...] I didn't want to just invent things, I also wanted to make the world better, and in order to do that, you need to do more than just invent things."[183] Such a vision drives many who are developing artificial intelligence. They believe they are serving humanity by making robotics that can solve our problems.

"Google was a company built on the values of its founders," discovered Peter Levy when spending time at "The Plex," Google's California headquarters. Larry Page and Sergey Brin "harbored ambitions to build a powerful corporation that would impact the entire world."[184]

One of their goals "was building a giant artificial intelligence machine that would bring uncertain consequences to the way all of us live. From the very beginning, its founders said

---

[182] Burfeind, *Gnostic America,* 53.
[183] Steven Levy, *In the Plex: How Google Thinks, Works, and Shapes Our Lives* (New York: Simon and Schuster, 2011) 11, 13.
[184] Levy, 5.

they wanted to change the world."[185] "From the very start, its founders saw Google as a vehicle to realize the dream of artificial intelligence in augmenting humanity."[186] They believed this could be fulfilled by making information available on the widest scale.

Jesus said, "The *truth* will make you free" (John 8:32). Google said, *information* will give you liberty. There is a profound difference between the respective promises. Jesus meant *qualitative* truth, while Page and Brin were thinking of *quantitative* data. The danger enters, however, when Google or any other internet source begins to twist information according to its own worldviews and values.

AI religion also has a "hope of heaven." This is the great quest driving the transhuman passion. It is not just a desire to enhance human performance in the here and now, but to do away with death itself. An article about PayPal Founder Peter Thiel begins with this editor's note:

> Billionaire Peter Thiel believes it all: Singularity, Convergence, Transcendence and most importantly, Transhumanism. In other words, Thiel wants to become immortal and live forever, essentially becoming a god. He is spending his billions to achieve it.[187]

Where will all of this lead? Those who cross the transhuman threshold and become immortal may discover that they have not stepped into Heaven but into Hell itself and dragged the rest of humanity down with them.

---

[185] Levy, 6.

[186] Levy, 6.

[187] "PayPal Founder Peter Thiel Is Pursuing Immortality With His Billions," By Jeff Bercovici, Technocracy.news, August 1, 2016. PayPal Founder Peter Thiel Is Pursuing Immortality With His Billions (technocracy. News)

So, even more than in 1939, we need "scientists of conscience" whose worldview is formed by ultimate truth and its values. There is a surprising example in a man who, like Albert Einstein, fled from Germany, but unlike Einstein, he used his science for a period to actually serve the Nazis. His story shows what happens when a person of science is transformed by True Transcendence.

CHAPTER 9

Flying with Von Braun

I find it best to accept God through faith,
as an intelligent will, perfect in goodness and wisdom,
revealing himself through creation.

—Werner von Braun

As a young man, Werner von Braun designed rockets for Hitler, but later in life, he encountered Christ and became a scientist with a conscience.

In 1972, I accompanied Harry Dent, my friend and boss at the White House, to NASA's Marshall Space Flight Center in Huntsville, Alabama.[188] Harry was the speaker at an event honoring NASA engineers. Following his talk, we boarded a NASA airplane to take Harry to his next engagement in Indianapolis and me on to Washington.

It would be one of the most memorable flights of my life.

---

[188] NASA is the National Aeronautics and Space Administration, the agency responsible for the United States space program.

139

A third person, also Washington-bound, joined Harry and me in the cabin of the government aircraft—Dr. Werner von Braun, considered by many to be the rocket scientist who thrust the United States into the age of space exploration.

Albert Einstein appeared early in this book, and it is fitting to speak of Von Braun in the final chapter. Like Einstein, Von Braun was a German and a physicist. There the resemblance ends. Einstein fled the Nazis, while Von Braun worked for them. In 1934, when Einstein left Germany and the monstrous Hitler regime was just getting its clawed foot into Germany's body politic, Von Braun graduated from the University of Berlin with a Ph.D. in physics. A decade later, he would be helping develop the V2 rockets with which Hitler blasted London and other cities.

Eventually, Von Braun became disenchanted with Hitler and the Nazis, and at one point, he protested the raining down of V2 rockets on innocent people. For that, he was locked in jail with some of his prime staff while Heinrich Himmler moved to take charge of the German rocket effort. However, the Nazis' missile development quickly began to fade, and Von Braun and his associates were released early in 1945 to get back to work.

By then, months after the June 6, 1944, Normandy Invasion, it was becoming evident to those who faced the facts that Germany was on its way to defeat. In the meantime, Von Braun was becoming a true scientist of conscience. He realized that German physicists would be taken by Soviet troops poised to invade Germany from the East and carried away into Russia to help it develop its rocket technology. Before that could happen, Von Braun and his whole staff surrendered to American troops. Some 500 scientists and their families were in that group.

Had Von Braun and his fellow rocket experts not made the decision to surrender themselves to the Americans, history might have been vastly different.

Professor Friedwart Winterberg wrote:

> It was Albert Einstein who changed our view of the universe to be a non-Euclidean curved space-time. [...] It was Werner von Braun who showed how to make the first step to take us into this universe, leaving the gravitational field of our planet earth. [...] Einstein's masterpiece is the general theory of relativity and gravitation, and Werner von Braun's masterpiece, the moon rocket.[189]

On that late-night flight in 1972, I tried to take in the enormity of the moment. The man in whose presence I sat was silent, and there was only the whoosh of the airplane engines. We landed in Indianapolis, Harry exited the aircraft, and I was alone in the cabin with Von Braun. The airplane had been reconfigured so that we sat in a lounge just outside the cockpit. I was sitting on a sofa, and Von Braun was on a big recliner across from me.

After we were again aloft, he pulled an impressive set of blueprints from his briefcase. I tried not to stare, but I could see that they had to do with the space shuttle then under development. President Richard Nixon had launched the space shuttle program in 1972, though the craft would not be launched until 1981.

---

[189] "Albert Einstein and Werner von Braun—The Two Great German-America Physicists Seen in a Historical Perspective," By Friedwart Winterberg, *Bulletin of the American Physical Society,* Volume 53, Number 5. Retrieved from http://meetings.aps.org/link/BAPS.2008.APR.T9.4.

The "Von Braun Paradigm" would be crucial in bringing about the historic event. The paradigm specified a sequence that would propel the United States into space, "Put a human in space," then "develop a reusable spacecraft." Next, "Use this vehicle to build a space station," then "inhabit the space station," utilizing it "as a base from which to launch manned expeditions to the moon, and then to Mars."

Though the full procedure was not used in getting astronauts to the moon and no human has stood on Mars (at this writing), nevertheless, the Von Braun Paradigm contributed much. President Nixon feared the full application would be too expensive for NASA's budget and trimmed it back, but the big outcome was the space shuttle.[190]

Ultimately, Von Braun became known as the "Father of Rocket Science."[191]

But there was another dimension to Von Braun. The man who had done so much to put humanity in space was profoundly aware of God and His transcendence. By the mid-1970s, Von Braun was in the clutch of the pancreatic cancer that would lead to his death in 1977. As he reflected on what he knew about the physical universe and the awesomeness of God, Von Braun yearned to see others know the oneness of science and faith. For him, science and faith "are like two windows in a house through which we look at the reality of the Creator and the laws manifested in his creation." Von Braun believed that as humans "see two different images through these two windows," they had "to keep trying to obtain a more complete and better integrated total picture of the ultimate

---

[190] https://www.space.com/12085-nasa-space-shuttle-history-born.html
[191] Ibid.

reality by properly tying together our scientific and religious concepts."[192]

Peering through those two windows, Von Braun was awed by God's majesty. "Finite man cannot begin to comprehend an omnipresent, omniscient, omnipotent, and infinite God," he thought. "I find it best to accept God through faith, as an intelligent will, perfect in goodness and wisdom, revealing himself through creation."[193]

When Von Braun died, Major General John Medaris said that Von Braun's:

> … imagination strolled easily among the stars, yet the farther out into the unknown and unknowable vastness of Creation his thoughts went, the more he was certain that the universe, and this small garden spot within it, came from no cosmic accident, but from the thought and purpose of an all-knowing God.[194]

In his earlier years, Von Braun would be noted for his unbelief with some of his friends even calling him the "merry heathen."[195] Von Braun had known about religion since his youth, but he came to know God personally in his adulthood. In 2004, a former NASA staff member, W. Albert Wilson, addressed the German Gideon Association. He told of Von Braun hearing him speak at an Alabama church and then

---

[192] Bergaust, E. 1976. *Werner von Braun.* Washington, DC: National Space Institute, 114

[193] Ernst Stuhlinger and Frederick I. Ordway III, *Werner von Braun: Crusader for Space: A Biographical Memoir*, Krieger Publishing Company: Malabar, Florida (1994)

[194] THEOLOGICAL DICTIONARY: Werner von Braun (tdwotd.blogspot. com)

[195] Stuhlinger and Ordway, 270.

receiving a call from Von Braun's assistant, asking Wilson to visit Von Braun in his office.

According to Wilson, Von Braun was deeply concerned about NASA and the space program, threatened by budget cuts. Wilson counseled Von Braun to seek God's guidance and then presented the Gospel to him. The great scientist, said Wilson, prayed and received Christ's salvation.

"When I left the office, I knew that he had become a Christian," said Wilson.[196]

Spiritual concerns had already been on Von Braun's mind. During the period in the 1960s when the Apollo program would take the first humans to the moon, "a new element began to surface in his conversations, and also in his speeches and his writings: a growing interest in religious thought," wrote Frederick Ordway.[197]

Von Braun's faith was not mere mysticism, but specifically grounded. Someone asked Von Braun what was in his mind when he signaled "go" for the Apollo 11 mission to the moon. "I quietly said the Lord's prayer," he replied.[198]

After Harry Dent deplaned that night in 1972, we took off for Washington. Not long after we were again in the air, Von Braun folded the blueprints he had been studying, tucked them neatly in his briefcase, and stood.

---

[196] "God Touches the Heart of a Scientist Through Gideons' Bible Ministry," By Eunice K.Y., *Christian Today,* May 28, 2004. Retrieved from https://www. christiantoday.com/article/god.touches.the.heart.of.a.scientist.through.gideons. bible.ministry./913.htm.

[197] Stuhlinger and Ordway, *op. cit.*

[198] http://www.ministers-best-friend.com/SCIENCE-Von-Braun-Inventor-of-Rockets-Great-Christian--COURSE-CRE-SCI-420.html

"I think I will drive now," he quipped in his precise German accent.

And with that, Von Braun stepped into the cockpit. My brief moment with an extraordinary man ended. However, through the decades and especially as my own faith deepened, I have reflected gratefully on the encounter with a person in whom science and faith came to be so beautifully integrated. In a way, that linkage had been unwittingly influenced by his mother in what might have been a prophetic act. When 13-year-old Werner was confirmed in the Lutheran church, her gift to her son was a telescope.

What Werner von Braun knew about the physics of the material universe helped humanity venture out into it; what Von Braun had come to understand about the Creator stirred in him an awe that even exceeded his admiration for Creation.

Such awe and the transformation it brings—as we have seen in Werner von Braun—are needed urgently in this age when new gods are being rolled off the assembly lines of the god factories at staggering speed.

"With no belief in higher meaning, too many young people turn to hook-up sex, drugs, and social media for fulfillment."

That was the opening claim in an article by Paul Vitz and Bruce Buff, *Adolescents in Crisis: Why We Need to Recover Religion.*[199] Vitz is professor emeritus of psychology at New York University, and Buff is a management consultant and information technology executive. "Our teenagers and often those still younger are taking their lives in increasing numbers,

---

[199] "Adolescents in Crisis: Why We Need to Recover Religion," By Paul Vitz and Bruce Buff, *National Review,* July 27, 2017. Retrieved from https://www.national-review.com/2017/07/teen-suicides-depression-anxiety-rising-religion-can-help/.

many seemingly without warning," say the authors. "Many more," they note, "are suffering from depression, anxiety, or related mental-health problems." There is a frequent linkage to social media, Vitz and Buff note.

This is happening at a time of economic prosperity. Some experts are blaming the crisis on "social media, smart phones, and school pressures." But Vitz and Buff believe it is deeper than that, "A far stronger case can be made for our society's decline in religious faith as the cause of these mental pathologies in our young." Vitz and Buff continue:

> In America, the transcendent dimension of life has historically been expressed primarily through the Judeo-Christian tradition, whose decline in recent years has created an enormous vacuum in meaning. This vacuum has been "filled" by postmodern nihilism combined with the "deconstruction"—aggressively taught in the academy—of belief in objective truth, goodness, and beauty. Moral relativism now eclipses transcendent meaning. The fragility of many young people—often termed "snowflakes"—shows their emotional vulnerability. They interpret ideas that challenge them as unbearable acts of aggression, and they use harsh and even violent measures to silence disagreeable opponents. In short, the prevalence of political correctness is a clear sign that belief in higher meaning and rational discussion has ceased to function in much of our higher-education system. Furthermore, political correctness is itself a symptom of the unstable mental condition of those who insist on it.

In their book, *Closer Together, Further Apart,* psychotherapist Robert Weiss and physician Jennifer P. Schneider explore "the effect of technology and the internet on parenting and work and relationships." While not ignoring the positive potentials of cyber development, including artificial intelligence, they are frank in presenting the challenges and dangers ahead.

Regarding sexual relationships and other forms of human interaction, they note:

> It is human nature to seek and/or create more refined sources of pleasure (refined cocaine, refined sugar, refined gaming and gambling via the internet, and so on), and if the most pleasurable sexual and/or romantic experience involves a computer or robot rather than an actual human being, so be it. [...] So, what is the future of dating, mating, sex, marriage, and parenting when computer-based interactions are simpler, more immediately available, and more pleasurable than being with a live person? Truthfully, only time will tell.[200]

"Only time will tell" may seem like an attitude of resignation, but that outlook might have spared the naïve rush to judgment by a man named Lincoln Steffens about events in his own time. In 1919, Steffens was a New York newspaper reporter who believed devoutly in socialism, and went to Russia that year to observe events there. The country was two years into the Bolshevik Revolution that had as its goal that of turning the world—starting with Russia and what became the Soviet Union—into a "workers' paradise."

Steffens proved himself one of the fathers of "fake news." After seeing the new Russia, he wrote, "I have seen the future, and it works!"

---

[200] Robert Weiss and Jennifer Schneider, *Closer Together, Farther Apart: The Effect of Technology and the Internet on Parenting, Work, and Relationships.* (Carefree, Arizona: Gentle Path Press, 2014), 103.

Like Weiss and Schneider now, Steffens should have taken a "time will tell" attitude, because time has indeed told the outcomes of Marxism. Steffens died in 1936 and did not get to see the future he thought he was observing in 1919. *The Black Book of Communism* reveals what that future looked like for millions slaughtered in the name of Marx:

- 65 million in the People's Republic of China
- 20 million in the Soviet Union
- 2 million in Cambodia
- 2 million in North Korea (and still rising as I write)
- 1.7 million in Ethiopia
- 1 million in the Eastern European countries once controlled by communists

I traveled in several Soviet Bloc countries not long after the collapse of communism in 1989-1990. I watched hopeless men line up every morning at kiosks to start their day with vodka. In one city, I stayed on the 15th floor of a Soviet-era apartment building and fretted every time I got on the elevator because the lightbulbs were snatched as soon as they were installed. I shopped in supermarkets whose shelves were mostly empty. As my flights taxied in at several airports, I saw the hulks of communist-era military aircraft rusting on the perimeters because they were still scavenged for parts to fit other airplanes and helicopters.

Steffens didn't see the future, but many others did.

Aleksandr Solzhenitsyn was one of them. He not only saw the future of his native country under the communists, but he experienced its horrors in its cruel prison system, the *gulag*. Eventually, Solzhenitsyn was released and made his way to America. In 1983, Solzhenitsyn was awarded the Templeton

Prize for Progress in Religion. His acceptance speech was titled, "Godlessness—the First Step to the Gulag." Solzhenitsyn said,

> Over a half century ago, while I was still a child, I recall hearing a number of old people offer the following explanation for the great disasters that had befallen Russia: "Men have forgotten God; that's why all this has happened." Since then, I have spent well-nigh 50 years working on the history of our revolution; in the process I have read hundreds of books, collected hundreds of personal testimonies, and have already contributed eight volumes of my own toward the effort of clearing away the rubble left by that upheaval. But if I were asked today to formulate as concisely as possible the main cause of the ruinous revolution that swallowed up some 60 million of our people, I could not put it more accurately than to repeat: "Men have forgotten God; that's why all this has happened."

In an age and culture in which people have once again forgotten God and His Transcendence, there should be grave concern, especially regarding technology and artificial intelligence. That's why the "scientists of conscience" have tried to warn us. It's not the technological advances themselves that we should fear, but the fact they are being developed without any regard for the transcendent—just like the communist societies of the 20th century.

But how can there be a revival of the transcendent vision, and what will be its source? The recovery must begin in churches. No other institutions in society are likely to even think about the issue, let alone raise it. There must be a rejoining of theology and science, not in a way that restricts scientific development but that provides scientific thought, research, development, and application with the broadest perspective.

Werner von Braun's gift of rocketry is an example. Infused with a renewed vision for God as the Transcendent One, Von Braun did not stop pursuing his field of science, but instead of Nazi or Soviet missiles that could destroy whole cities, Von Braun focused on rockets that could lift human beings to the moon and bring them back.

Von Braun and his science that once brought destruction and misery ultimately was used for good. Because of his view of God as transcendent over the universe and the science that sought to understand it, Von Braun moved from his youthful *hubris* to a state of hope.

Von Braun would impact other scientists with the vision of pursuing knowledge with a perspective of expectancy raised by their consciousness of God's transcendence. One of those scholars is Dr. Otis Graf, a technical advisor on this book.

The Transformational Church

I left the White House in 1973, after almost three years of service there in one of the American presidency's most turbulent periods. In many ways, I was disillusioned and hopeless about the future of civilization. Though I thought I had forever abandoned a call to church ministry, there was a conviction growing within me. After watching government and other institutions struggle to sustain civilization and solve rapidly surmounting problems, I was beginning to realize that *the pivotal agency in society is the church.*

Institutions and movements can incite revolution, but revolutionary movements work from the outside in. That is, they can force acquiescence to their principles and changes, but maintaining the new status quo established by the revolution requires the tight control of magnitudes of laws and regulations and their enforcement.

The authentic biblical church (and not everything that calls itself "church" is that), however, is an agency of transformation. It is the embassy of the Kingdom of Heaven in the fallen world (2 Corinthians 5:20). That Kingdom, said Jesus, is catalytic (Matthew 13:33). In contrast to mere revolution, transformation works from "inward to outward"—from the Holy Spirit's interaction with the human spirit outward through soul and body. What is inside is ultimately "worked out" (Philippians 2:12).

Churches must recognize that the concerns about artificial intelligence constitute *spiritual* issues. This is especially the church's turf. Who or what institution in society will even raise the question of transcendence but the church? Who knows the dynamics of transcendence and the sound doctrines regarding transcendence but the church?

"This is not a problem for government policy," say Vitz and Buff, as they contemplate the challenge to teens in the computer age. In fact, they write, "government just needs to get out of the way—and be less hostile to religion." They point out:

> While the secular class and those victimized by their policies have been shedding their religious beliefs, evidence for the positive effects of religious life have been repeatedly reported by many studies over the past decades. Many of them show that strongly religious people are happier, healthier, and live longer than those with no religious belief and practice. Having faith in God and attributing a religious meaning to life anchors people, directs their efforts to things beyond the material world, protects them against setbacks, and provides supportive community.

The church must not be anti-artificial intelligence, but it must be the voice in society that asks the hard questions and gives true answers. The church must take the prophetic stance in society, even though this may keep her unwelcome. But she must proclaim God's majestic holiness and transcendence and live it in the midst of society.

Jesus Christ's Great Commission to His church was to go into all the world under and upon the strength of His all-encompassing authority "and make disciples of all nations, baptizing them in the name of the Father and the Son and the Holy Spirit, teaching them to observe all I have commanded you; and lo, I am with you always, even to the end of the age" (Matthew 28:18-20).

A "disciple" is a "learner." The first thing the church should teach its learners is the transcendence of God. We saw in Chapter Two how the focus on God as the Most High has faded into an obsession with the immanent, beginning with self. If churches do not bring back the transcendent focus, there is no other institution that will. Cultures are sliding fast into the authoritarianism of human philosophies with institutions and individuals taking on the garb of a false transcendence.

That brings us back to the important distinctions between knowledge and wisdom.

1. Knowledge is knowing many details about the subject.
2. Wisdom is knowing what to do with that knowledge.
3. Knowledge is quantitative.
4. Wisdom is qualitative.
5. Knowledge without wisdom can lead to destructive ends.
6. Wisdom without knowledge is pretense.
7. Transcendence links knowledge and wisdom.

In the fact of the coming gods being built and programmed by human beings who have little or no regard for True

Transcendence, this is not an advance upward but a death spiral for humanity.

Werner von Braun made his decision to surrender to the West because he knew a fundamental rule of science: It will go where it will and as far as possible. The "fallacy of technology," writes Richard M. Weaver, is the idea that "because a thing can be done, it must be done." This notion dominates science to the point the technical expertise is absorbed totally and "becomes blind to the very concept of ends."[201] Yet we cannot place boundaries on the pursuit of knowledge and inventiveness. However, we must recover the awareness of Transcendence that makes us accountable for the way we use our knowledge, as Von Braun ultimately did.

The Bible verse on his grave proves it:

> The heavens declare the glory of God;
> And the firmament showeth His handiwork.
> (Psalm 19:1)

Who, then, will rule the coming gods?

The answer is the truly transcendent Lord of lords and King of kings revealed in the written Word, the Bible, and the incarnate Word—Jesus, the Christ.

There are important actions churches must implement to help revive the focus on God and His transcendence. They must:

---

[201] Richard M. Weaver, *Ideas Have Consequences* (Chicago: University of Chicago Press, 1948), 60. Cited in Olsen, *The Turn to Transcendence*, 3.

1. Prepare church leaders for a vital role in confronting the false gospel of the transcendent machine through seminaries and other theological institutions.
2. Teach and/or preach the theology of the attributes of God, emphasizing His transcendent holiness and majesty.
3. Restore the idea and practice of *reverence* and its extension into all of life.
4. Help people understand the reality of sin and its consequences (ultimately, Hell).
5. Increase understanding of the futility of true progress apart from God.
6. Connect people with the tragic history of humans pretending to transcendence.
7. Return an emphasis on the fear of God and accountability to Him as the ultimate Authority.
8. Develop an understanding and appreciation for the immensity of Christ's incarnation and His sacrifice.
9. Make disciples.
10. Recover worship of God's transcendent majesty.

CPSIA information can be obtained
at www.ICGtesting.com
Printed in the USA
BVHW031156191021
619310BV00011B/52